MACMILLAN MODERN DRAMATISTS

Modern Dramatists
Series Editors: *Bruce and Adele King*

Published titles

Further titles in preparation

PETER SHAFFER

C. J. Gianakaris
Professor of English and Theatre
Western Michigan University

MACMILLAN

First published 1992

Published by
THE MACMILLAN PRESS LTD
Houndmills, Basingstoke, Hampshire RG21 2XS
and London
Companies and representatives
throughout the world

Printed in Hong Kong

EG0S8 36

E~03785

822.92

British Library Cataloguing in Publication Data
Gianakaris, C. J.
Peter Shaffer.—(Macmillan modern dramatists)
I. Title   II. Series
822
ISBN 0–333–41372–5 (hc)
ISBN 0–333–41373–3 (pbk)

Contents

Editors' Preface

The *Modern Dramatists* series is an international collection of introductions to major and significant nineteenth- and twentieth-century dramatists, movements and new forms of drama in Europe, Great Britain, America and new nations such as Nigeria and Trinidad. Besides new studies of great and influential dramatists of the past, the series includes volumes on contemporary authors, recent trends in the theatre and on many dramatists, such as writers of farce, who have created theatre 'classics' while being neglected by literary criticism. The volumes in the series devoted to individual dramatists include a biography, a survey of the plays, and detailed analysis of the most significant plays, along with discussion, where relevant, of the political, social, historical and theatrical context. The authors of the volumes, who are involved with theatre as playwrights, directors, actors, teachers and critics, are concerned with the plays as theatre and discuss such matters as performance, character interpretation and staging, along with themes and context.

BRUCE KING
ADELE KING

Acknowledgements

The author and publishers wish to thank the following for permission to use copyright material.

André Deutsch Ltd, for the extracts from *Amadeus*, *Lettice and Lovage* and *Yonadab* by Peter Shaffer.

Every effort has been made to trace all the copyright holders, but if any have been inadvertently overlooked the publishers will be pleased to make the necessary arrangement at the first opportunity.

1
Peter Shaffer and his Early Career: The Novels and Broadcast Plays

Peter Shaffer, the Man

British playwright Peter Shaffer represents a rare breed becoming even rarer as the twenty-first century approaches: a writer for the stage who combines verbal articulateness with exceptional theatrical inventiveness. Since his first stage play, *Five Finger Exercise*, appeared in 1958, Shaffer has grown into giant prominence in the world of theatre. The mainstay of his reputation is a series of philosophically probing dramas: *The Royal Hunt of the Sun* (1964), *Equus* (1973), *Shrivings* (1970, 1974), *Amadeus* (1979) and *Yonadab* (1985). But there also are dazzling comedies and satires as well, such as the one-act comedies *The Private Ear*/*The Public Eye* (1962), *Black Comedy* (1965) and *White Liars* (1967) and the full-length

1

Lettice & Lovage (1987). When considered together, Peter Shaffer's stage works comprise as varied and entertaining a one-man repertoire as is available today.

His abiding popularity is evidenced by impressive box-office figures, enthusiastic reviews and countless top awards. The appeal of Shaffer's work is so wide that it has inspired adaptations in ballet (*Equus*) and opera (*Royal Hunt*). *Equus* and *Amadeus* won Tony Awards, and *Amadeus* in its film format earned eight Academy Awards in 1984, including Best Picture and Best Screenplay (also written by Shaffer). Movies made of his plays are a sore point with Shaffer, however. Other film adaptations – *Five Finger Exercise*, *The Public Eye* and *Royal Hunt* – range from competent to dreadful. Notwithstanding the extraordinary success of the movie *Amadeus*, Shaffer remains sceptical about transferring drama to the screen, particularly since Sidney Lumet's literalised film version of *Equus*.

Shaffer's individual style accrues from a union of diverse writing strengths. His mastery of language is impressive, and his mature plays overflow with elegant, memorable dialogue. Few writers for the theatre today exhibit a comparable sensitivity with language, though Shaffer early in his career revealed a proclivity for overwrought and sentimental verbiage. Shaffer's principal characteristic, however, is his story-telling ability, which has found expression in a wide diversity of works, ranging from well-made plays to epic spectacle. These are also structurally very different from each other, and he continues to explore new directions in theatrical expression. The serious dramas in particular incorporate inventive, even experimental, stage tactics such as epic and 'total theatre' – styles rarely seen in mainstream theatre. Playgoers may recognise elements of Ibsen, Shaw and Osborne in Shaffer's work, as well as glints of Brecht, Wilder and Artaud. Neither a naturalist nor an absurdist, he has combined richly variegated means to arrive at an individual dramatic identity.

Shaffer builds drama on profound human issues, avoiding the fluff that pervades much popular theatre. His favoured theme implies a conjunction of metaphysical puzzles: does a universal deity exist in our unjust world, and, if so, what is man's relationship to him? If no god exists, how does man infer an order through which to lead a satisfying life? Shaffer expects no easy answers to the questions that he poses, but prefers to raise them rather than pretend that they are not there. His dramas are means to scan the universal experience for clarification about the human condition. Except occasionally in the comedies, his dramatic parables inevitably conclude on a sceptical note. Shaffer's protagonists *almost* corner the elusive god sought in each play, but remain stymied when no evidence appears with which to confirm that god's existence. Walter Langer's idealism in *Five Finger Exercise* is ultimately shown to be misguided; Pizarro's momentary show of faith in *Royal Hunt of the Sun* leads to profound disillusionment; Dysart in the last analysis conspires with society in *Equus* to seal off Alan's personal god; Mozart and Salieri in *Amadeus* fail to receive just 'compensation' from God, the one during his lifetime and the other after; Yonadab futilely tries to create his own version of godhead among mortals. Shaffer's searching hero is not Rousseau's innocent Candide but Camus's existential Meursaut instead. Scholars of religions particularly appreciate the unique perspective resulting from Shaffer's concerns with contemporary thought. Larry D. Bouchard believes, 'The shards of a broken cultural order, in isolation and in new juxtapositions, illuminate

3

reality by an oddly refracted light. Shaffer's characters come to recognize little hierophanies, not a single enlightening epiphany. Shaffer would be a metaphysician of the provisional, an ontologist whose integrity is tested by his refusal either to claim being or to assent to its absence'[1]. Few other dramatists today would risk losing a Broadway venue with plays like Shaffer's which stretch the audience's thought-capabilities – and then end the plots with pessimistic resolutions. As *Amadeus* shows clearly, it is his adept comic irony that retains the audience's loyalty when they are faced with Shaffer's unprettified view of the universe.

To emphasise the pessimism is seriously misleading, however. Shaffer's half-dozen delightful comedies capture the social foibles of our age, ranging from romantic miscues to bureaucratic fumbling. Shaffer's early comedies chronicled the laughable misadventures of young love. More recently, characters such as Lotte and Lettice reflect a mature illusionlessness; society's strictures for them inhibit and restrict, and they must trust their own judgement without awaiting outside guidance either from the community or from an absent deity. Viewed broadly, then, Shaffer's is a vivifying imagination incorporating themes of intellectual inquiry expressed often through non-traditional theatrical techniques.[2]

At the same time it must be said that his balancing act between intellectualised drama and Broadway or West End conventions has been maintained at a price. Because he is not firmly installed in either the commercial camp or that of the avant-garde, Shaffer remains suspect in the eyes of both factions. In the view of a few fashionable 'intellectuals' he is a lackey of Broadway interests, using brilliance of staging to blind audiences to mundane notions. The very popularity of his plays is taken as proof

that he panders to a mass audience. For such critics
Shaffer is just an able craftsman, not a blazing leader in
the theatrical trade. Other opinionated observers comp-
lain of Shaffer's unfair advantage over most commercially
successful dramatists because his plays are usually developed under the aegis of non-profit organisations, the
British National Theatre in particular. Only after being
nurtured in elitist theatrical incubators (at public expense)
are his plays transferred to a commercial forum, they
assert. Shaffer thus finds himself caught between opposing
theatrical camps, receiving some hostile critical salvos
along with the Tonys and Oscars.[3] Over the years he has
learned to ignore gratuitous detractors who attack him for
being on the 'wrong' side, though such unwarranted
sniping has had its psychic effects. Neither in his personal
nor in his professional life does Shaffer now suffer fools
readily. Because his plays tend to evoke varied and
contradictory responses, one of the objectives of this book
must be to find out why this is, from the plays themselves.

Shaffer brings to his work both the intellectual *données*
of his own era and a highly personal perspective on being
human in this world. One consequence is that the author
of such thoughtful psychological drama as *Five Finger
Exercise*, *The Royal Hunt of the Sun*, *Equus*, *Shrivings*,
Amadeus and *Yonadab* is also capable of producing
sparkling satires such as *The Private Ear*, *The Public Eye*,
Black Comedy, *White Liars* and *Lettice & Lovage*, in
which keen wit addresses social malfeasance. Nor is there
anything stereotyped in his approach: his plays range from
nearly pristine naturalism in *Five Finger Exercise* to
stylised 'Total Theatre' in *The Royal Hunt of the the Sun*
and *Yonadab*. Farce, drama, realistic 'well-made plays'
and presentational symbolism – all these dramatic
approaches find expression in his writings.

5

Peter Levin Shaffer was born into an Orthodox Jewish home in Liverpool, England, on 15 May 1926 – a few minutes after his identical twin brother Anthony. A third son, Brian, was born to the Shaffers a few years later. Interestingly, though Brian began his professional life as a scientist, all three brothers ultimately were to pursue careers in writing and in the arts. Their father, Jack, was a North Countryman with a property business; their mother, Reka, originally came from Devonport. The children attended preparatory school in Liverpool until the family moved to London in 1936. The Shaffer twins attended St Paul's School before the Second World War intervened. St Paul's, Shaffer acknowledges, offered him a fine education. There also was opportunity for piano lessons while growing up, and he mastered that instrument far beyond average competence. That factor helps explain the exceptional and intelligent use of music in *Amadeus* and several of his other plays.

No university training was available, however, before he completed national service. Because of bad eyes, Shaffer could not serve in Britain's armed forces, and instead he was conscripted as a 'Bevin Boy' to work underground in the Chislet colliery in Kent from 1944 to 1947. In 1947 both Shaffer twins matriculated at Cambridge, where Peter read history and co-edited the university magazine *Granta* with his brother. Upon graduating in 1950 at the age of twenty-four, Peter Shaffer felt the pull of both literature and theatre; yet he resisted that impulse, considering a writing career somehow unrespectable. He took on a series of jobs in the business world after an unsuccessful search for employment with London publishing houses. From 1951 until 1954 he lived in New York City, where his places of employment included a department store, an airlines terminal and the New York

Public Library. After returning to London he worked for
the music publisher Boosey and Hawkes. Shaffer also
became literary critic and reviewer for the weekly *Truth* in
1956. But none of these jobs gave him the satisfaction
required for a lifetime commitment, and, as he told Brian
Connell in an interview, during the early 1950s he decided
to try for a literary career, writing in a genre that we may
now find rather surprising.[4]

The Detective Novels

Peter Shaffer's writing career did not begin in the theatre
but with three detective novels. Those books today provide interest for the curious but reveal few hints of the stage
successes to follow. In 1951, at the age of twenty-five,
Shaffer published *The Woman in the Wardrobe* under the
pseudonym Peter Antony. An exciting but thoroughly
conventional mystery seasoned with ironic humour, it
soon was followed by two similar suspense novels, *How
Doth the Little Crocodile?* (1952) and *Withered Murder*
(1955).[5] The last two works were written jointly by Peter
and his twin brother Anthony, destined to become an
award-winning playwright in his own right with *Sleuth*.
According to Peter, the brothers worked on the books
following an informal system whereby one would lay out
the basic plot while the other filled in narrative and
dialogue. In most essential features, the novels are conventional detective stories. They share a basic structural
framework, as all three plots centre on a renowned
investigator who stumbles onto the scene of an unsolved
murder. Esteemed for their investigatory shrewdness, the
detectives (called Verity in the first two books and Fathom
in the last) are enlisted to help solve hideous crimes. In each

case the victim is described as despicable, with numerous enemies, thereby providing each plot with abundant murder suspects. The master investigator sorts through the numerous leads – mostly false ones – until he develops a surprise theory which accommodates the bewildering facts. Finally, in all three tales the astute sleuth, after assembling the suspects to create a court room situation, singles out the culprit to solve the case.

The Woman in the Wardrobe provides the plot template. The engaging central protagonist is Mr Verity, whose name mirrors his consuming passion for the truth. Described as an 'immense man, just tall enough to carry his breadth majestically', Verity is an erstwhile solver of crimes, and definitely not the ordinary detective for hire. Shaffer employs a standard omniscient narrator to focus on Verity. The chase itself, not moral or legal imperatives, most attracts him. Shaffer cultivates in Verity a zeal for working out puzzles and conundrums, a characteristic observable in many of the playwright's subsequent dramatic characters.

Amnestie, a fictitious village outside London, is the site of most of the action. Verity happens to see someone crawling furtively from one window to another along the upper ledge of the notorious Hotel Charter. While reporting what he has seen to the hotel management, Verity meets the suspect climber, now spattered with blood. Another bloodied character is hauled into the hotel by the local constable amid confusion and exclamations about a murder. Everyone marches upstairs to the room where the alleged murder has occurred. But the door is locked from the inside, and Verity borrows the constable's revolver to shoot the lock open. All enter to find Maxwell, the occupant of the room, laying dead near the door. He has been shot. A hotel maid found locked in the wardrobe tells a fantastic tale of a masked man breaking into the room to shoot Maxwell just as she was serving him breakfast. Verity's investigations confirm that Maxwell had blackmailed nearly everyone at the hotel, providing numerous suspects with solid motives – and opportunities – for murder. Yet the miscellaneous details do not fit together, and the remainder of the novel traces Verity's search for better answers. Eventually he uncovers the facts regarding Maxwell's death: none of the apparent suspects is guilty.

The Woman in the Wardrobe carves out little fresh territory as suspense fiction. Shaffer's contributions to the genre lie in the startling resolution and in the fully delineated characters, who generate above-average interest. From the beginning of his writing career Shaffer showed a gift for inventing characters with colourful eccentricities. Verity is a man of unusual appearance with a wry wit that will remind playgoers of the cutting satire of such later figures as Salieri, Yonadab and Lotte Schoen. Moreover, the novel's outrageous early scene in which suspects crawl in and out of windows and closets hints at the broad physical farce later perfected in *Black Comedy* and *Lettice & Lovage*. The novel's subtitle is, appropriately, 'A Light-hearted Detective Story', and *The Woman in the Wardrobe* has the lightest tone of the three mysteries. Adding to the levity are the book's amusing caricatures drawn by Nicolas Bentley. Humour leavens Shaffer's writing from the outset.

Shaffer's first collaboration with his brother Anthony was *How Doth the Little Crocodile?* The subtitle, 'A Mr Verity Detective Story', indicates the authors' intention to continue the Verity series, and the hero now is further individualised as a corpulent white-haired fellow in his sixties sporting a Van Dyck goatee and a black Cuban cigar. He exhibits a compulsion to collect artifacts from far-off lands. *How Doth the Little Crocodile?* is darker than the first novel, even though its title derives from Lewis Carroll's *Alice in Wonderland*. Nastiness permeates the story, and the plot overflows with malicious characters performing disgusting deeds.

While relaxing at the Beverly Club, an exclusive men's retreat in London, Verity discusses with his fellow members the recent murder of their colleague Sir Derek Livingston, an eminent jurist. The club members eventually persuade Verity to investigate the case. The remainder of the action (except for the ultimate resolution) occurs at Livingston's estate outside London and at the Harp Hotel nearby. Like *The Woman in the Wardrobe* this mystery features a total cad as murder victim. Livingston's unforgivable treatment of his wife, his mistress, his sole blood heir (a nephew) and his former friends had turned them all against him. Verity's methodical enquiries produce many suspects, all with roughly equal motive and opportunity, and the evidence does not single out any of them. The Shaffers set the story's final showdown back in the Beverly Club, where the numerous suspects and other interested parties gather to hear the results of Verity's findings. There, in what is typical of the Shafferian murder novels, an astonishing exposé occurs: Lord Livingston had cynically planned his own death. Moreover, he deliberately planted false evidence to implicate innocent suspects – all to achieve 'the perfect crime', which became Livingston's paramount goal after learning that he was dying of an untreatable disease.

Withered Murder, the last of Peter Shaffer's suspense novels (also co-authored with Anthony), is the most imaginative of all, with many engrossing characters and ingenious plot twists. By this point in their writing the

Shaffer brothers had developed a taut narrative style that propels the story forward swiftly and surely. The hostile relationships between characters and the frequent verbal allusions to the 'night of horror at Crab Point' and to 'the night of terror almost done' contribute to a pervasive sense of foreboding. Cruel acts and gory killings occur throughout the book to create an aura of limitless evil. The book's title derives from *Macbeth*, one of Shakespeare's bloodiest tragedies, and gruesome lines taken from that play precede each chapter as epigraphs. Imminent death becomes the chief motif, voiced early and often by the story's detective raisonneur, here called Mr Fathom. Even before the plot complications begin, he muses aloud, *'Why do I know that someone is going to die?'*[6]

By setting the story on an almost inaccessible island, the authors evoke an intense claustrophobia. Because travel to the mainland must be arranged in advance, the inmates of the island hotel are all conscious of their isolation. And, given the numerous antagonisms among the island residents, who find it difficult to avoid each other, tensions increase steadily. Violence and cruelty dominate the plot. The presumed murder victim, Celia Whitley, is again a vicious character, hated by many. Some of the story's effects are of a type usually associated with the horror genre, as in this description of a mutilated corpse: 'Miss Celia Whitley lay on her back on the thick carpet, the brilliant red evening dress wrapped about her, and stained with a deeper red. She had no face. The flesh had been ripped and clawed away: her eyes too were damaged: even her grey hair was rich with blood and lay tangled in the sockets.'

Blackmail, jealousy, fear and greed all play a part in the homicides uncovered in *Withered Murder*. The result is a misanthropy more evocative of Anthony Shaffer's subsequent detective drama (written for stage and film) than of his brother's plays. Systematically, through uncanny sensitivity to people's use of subterfuge, Fathom unlocks the puzzles in the plot to reach an outcome more shocking than in either of the other novels. Again, the familiar resolution scene occurs: Fathom commences slowly and methodically, specifying why the prime suspects cannot be guilty of murder. Only one person – finally – can be the true culprit.

In an extraordinary turnabout, the murderer is revealed to be Miss Whitley, the presumed victim. An innocent older woman was sacrificed – drugged, then slain – by Miss Whitley, who then took on a disguise. The need to deface the corpse becomes clear once the substitution has been revealed. Fathom uncovers an intricate plan in which Miss Whitley pretended to have been killed by her secretary, Hilary Stanton, who in turn died, apparently by suicide. The stunned assembly at the hotel hears Fathom's explanation for the scheme. Miss Whitley through blackmail had forced the pretty Hilary Stanton to become her lesbian lover, but, when the younger woman insisted on leaving to get married, the jealous and rejected Whitley concocted a bizarre plan to retaliate. Fathom's exposé before the hotel guests flushes out the disguised Whitley, who suddenly rushes from the room. Climbing the stairs to an upper-floor window, she leaps to her death on the patio below.

The three 'whodunits' written wholly or partly by Peter Shaffer suggest him to be an adroit writer who clearly enjoys the elements making up standard detective fare. In each of these books interest centres on the chief protagonist. Verity and Fathom receive colourful attributes that impress them on the reader's memory. No psychological insights are provided for most other characters, however, and they assume roles as pawns. The unexpected dénouement of each novel is striking and original. But the concluding scene, with all possible suspects brought together, is entirely conventional. Agatha Christie and countless other suspense writers regularly use the same pattern. Readers might reasonably suspect that the Shaffers are parodying the shopworn 'court-room' technique – i.e., climactic 'verdict' boldly announced before gasping court witnesses. The ironic tone of all three novels makes this at least a plausible interpretation.

The temptation to see the suspense novels as foreshadowing characteristics of Peter Shaffer's plays must not be over-indulged. Whereas murder mysteries have been the staple of his brother Anthony's successful career in theatre and film,[7] Peter Shaffer's later work is more diverse, and echoes of the early detective tales are correspondingly fewer. The central figure in Shaffer's one-act comedy *The Public Eye*, Julian Christoforou, is labelled a private detective, but he is a wholly unorthodox one: a gregarious sleuth whose purview is the human heart. His investigations ferret out the problems in a romantic dilemma, and his solutions help to recement a foundering marriage. Another example is Martin Dysart, the psychiatrist in *Equus*, who functions as a detective in relation to the ailing psyche of Alan Strang. Instead of tracking down external leads, Dysart delves ever deeper into the spiritual and psychological make-up of the troubled lad, until he uncovers the underlying mystery of Strang's bizarre behaviour. Even Antonio Salieri functions partly as a detective. As our narrative guide in *Amadeus*, he aims to ascertain facts – from his own perspective – about Mozart's life and premature death. The central question, as he aptly phrases it early in the play, is '*The Death of Mozart, – or, Did I do It?*'

Yet, unlike detective tales, Peter Shaffer's plays are not primarily concerned with surface events. They focus on crucial interior enigmas generated in the story. Each play is erected on a critical puzzle that evokes immediate and persistent suspense. Shaffer's plots feature protagonists digging relentlessly for information – 'evidence' – to help solve the central riddle. It is a pattern repeated in nearly all his serious dramas.[8] Shaffer's investigative approach in the plays is a variation on the search motif associated with rites of passage, because by solving the underlying riddle the hero gains knowledge concerning himself and life generally. In seeking to unravel the magical powers of Atahuallpa, for instance, Pizarro must examine the Inca king's concepts and values. In that play's resolution, Pizarro comes face to face with a bleak vision of human mortality. The chief action in *Shrivings* similarly invalidates an idealised perception of human life, though more vaguely expressed. When Sir Gideon Petrie, who is portrayed as a celebrated peace activist, loses his wager to the cynic Mark Askelon, the deceptions underlying Gideon's altruism surface. In *Equus*, Dysart tracks down the workings of Alan's mind and soul, only to discover an irreconcilable chasm between individual spontaneity and social strictures in his own life.

Shaffer's mystery novels are best viewed as intellectual conundrums, demonstrating the cool detachment of objective exercises. His dramas, even when evincing attributes of suspense fiction, focus on moral and metaphysical enigmas. The following chapters explore the ethical issues raised in each play to reveal a common element: the protagonist's search to define a relationship between humankind and a universal deity. Except in his comedies, this search dominates Shaffer's playwriting. The three 'whodunits' alert us to his abiding taste for suspenseful themes, but, after these initial excursions into narrative prose, Shaffer concentrated all his efforts on drama, never again to return to the novel as his medium.

Radio and Television Plays

Three years separated Shaffer's last mystery novel and *Five Finger Exercise*, his first commercial stage success. During that interval, from 1955 to 1958 and briefly thereafter, he wrote for radio and television. Both broadcast media were thriving, and, as is still the case, it was common for fledgling playwrights in Great Britain to write for the networks, public and private. Other British dramatists who have written for television and radio at some stage in their careers include Harold Pinter, Tom Stoppard, John Osborne, David Hare, Simon Gray, Michael Frayn, Joe Orton and Peter Nichols.[9]

The first of Shaffer's four broadcast pieces was the drama *The Salt Land*, produced by Independent Television (ITV) in 1955. A BBC radio drama called *The Prodigal Father* followed in 1957, and a second television play, *Balance of Terror*, was broadcast by the BBC the same year. Not until 1989 did Shaffer return to the air, then with a one-person radio play called *Whom Do I Have the Honour of Addressing*? Thematically, all four works concern issues from contemporary life, and the early works are particulary concerned with the difficulty of balancing historical values from the past with those of the present. These early broadcast pieces confirm Shaffer's deep interest in historical matters, already evident from numerous historical allusions in the novels, and are all set in post-Second World War Europe. The British approach to ruling, built on a social hierarchy overseen by the gentility, had succeeded for centuries. But after two world wars the system clearly no longer worked. The torch passed to the United States with its more ample resources. That event raised hard questions in the minds of many European intellectuals. Shaffer's early works often refer to the contrast between the strong though culturally retrogressive United States and the tradition-rich but enervated British. At that point in his writing career he was concentrating on matters involving contemporary life. Period dramas would come later.

Stylistically, these first plays rely on the conventional social realism then dominating British drama. As a new explorer of the medium, Shaffer worked conservatively, and no radical or revelatory techniques are observable within these first plays. Still, two characteristics associated with his later writing are prefigured in his early work, suggesting at the outset a promising talent for playwriting. First is an intuitive dramatic sense whereby compelling characters are brought into conflict over significant issues. In every play Peter Shaffer has written, a clear-cut antagonism between characters provides a centrepoint of conflict to assure that dramatic tension never lags. Second is his talent for virile dialogue to provide impetus to events in the plot. Comparing his novels with the television and radio dramas, one instantly perceives how much more liberated Shaffer's writing becomes when addressing the requirements of the dramatic medium. Because Shaffer shapes stories as a head-on collision of wills, his more natural artistic home lies within the theatre, with its potential for presenting such a collision directly.

The Salt Land, shown on ITV on 8 November 1955, was initially meant for the stage, but, because of its uncomplicated realism and its timely subject, the script (never formally published) readily lent itself to television adaptation when no opportunity for a theatre staging presented itself. The two-act drama is set during the critical period from autumn 1947 to late summer 1949, when Great Britain under United Nations mandate removed its peace-keeping soldiers from part of Palestine, allowing the formation of the state of Israel. Violence erupted at once, leading to the first Arab–Israeli war. The birth of modern Israel proved a momentous cultural and historical event, and *The Salt Land* draws on the intense emotions generated. Shaffer's dual plot concerns the antagonisms within a fictional refugee family in the new land, and the lethal larger conflagration of the Arab–Israeli struggle. It is within the story of the Mayer family that metaphysical questions are considered. Like so many of his later dramas, *The Salt Land* manifests Shaffer's persistent search for an identifiable force governing the universe and providing some rationale for events that otherwise seem wholly unjust.

As the play begins, a dozen fugitive Jews are shown crowded on a small boat heading for a clandestine landing on the Palestine coast. The mood is anxious; any noise could alert the circling patrol boats to the presence of the illicit vessel. If captured, the Jews would be returned to a hostile Europe which already had betrayed them during the Second World War. The patriarchal figure among the refugees is a middle-aged German businessman named Mayer, who, with his sons Arieh and Jo, invests his last hopes in the territory promised the world's exiled Jews. Jewish himself and a witness to the true-life UN maneouvres, Shaffer dramatically explores the motives of participants in this great migration. Arieh and Jo incarnate wholly disparate expectations of the new life awaiting them in their new home. For Arieh, a religious fundamentalist, Israel represents the culmination of a sacred biblical adventure, a chance to create the Promised Land described in the Talmud. For Jo, an 'operator' familiar with every deception for making a fast buck, the new land represents limitless opportunities for cheating the gullible settlers.

Shaffer frames the intense metaphysical war between these two brothers against the action-filled backdrop of a fledgling nation fighting implacable enemies. The three detective novels never touch comparable issues of philosophy and metaphysics, and these early plays mark a measurable move forward in Shaffer's writing. Not only are the themes weighty and effectively developed, but the characters are far more complex than the entertaining but formulaic personages in the mystery novels. The Mayer brothers delineate their contrasting personalities and outlooks through Shaffer's forceful dialogue.

We also encounter for the first time the archetype of duelling protagonists, the pattern dominating all Shaffer's stage dramas. Two basic attributes in human nature – most simply described as instinct and reason – will ripen into full-blown, complex versions of Apollonian and Dionysian dualities in *Equus* and *Amadeus*.[10] Qualities reflecting these basic psychic tensions are adumbrated in the Mayer brothers. Inverse images of each other, Jo and Arieh live through (and respond to) the arduous birth of Israel. The elder brother, Arieh, advocates unquestioning support of the omnipotent God set forth in Jewish scripture. His spiritual lodestone stems from an instinctual belief which defies 'pure' logic. Despite evidence that their kibbutz will be overrun by enemy Palestinians, Arieh with self-righteous certitude insists, 'We will all be delivered in God's own time . . . Without God, nothing is possible.' Jo, meantime, sneeringly taunts Arieh, 'According to him and his precious Talmud we are to do nothing at all. Just sit down and wait to be butchered. Such a comforting philosophy.'

It is a classic Shafferian conundrum: neither Arieh's idealistic spirituality nor Jo's opportunistic pragmatism can succeed without the other in the violent crucible called Israel. Jo's tainted money, we learn, paid for the Mayers' boat passage to the Promised Land. Furthermore, it is Jo's secret support which permits Arieh's struggling community to receive the arms and food supplies it needs for survival. Reluctantly, Arieh accepts Jo's blood money in order to realise his life's goal of leading his people to a new, better life. But, if Arieh is to remain Israel's bright miracle-worker, he must betray the ideals underlying his beloved nation. The price Jo asks of Arieh is control of the political instruments in the fledgling country. Pride is Arieh's downfall; he bows to Jo's demands in exchange for prosperity and the political success it brings. Shaffer calls *The Salt Land* a modern tragedy because Arieh, an exceptional but flawed man, is ultimately destroyed by pride.[11] Yet, as in traditional tragedy, the protagonist experiences *cognitio* as well as *agon*. Shaffer writes a theatrically gripping climax in which Arieh tries to reverse his moral decline. In an effort to salvage remnants of his self-esteem, the disillusioned zealot attempts a total exorcism which ends the life of Jo and ruins his own. Shaffer distinguishes the brothers markedly, and by focusing on the central philosophical conflict dividing them he allows the highly charged resolution to emerge logically from earlier events. Sometimes, however, an overwrought diction prefigures Shaffer's tendency to overwrite emotionally charged scenes – a trait that may be observed even in his finest dramas. Of course, a proper assessment of the play's strengths depends on witnessing a performance, and ITV has said that its production of *The Salt*

Land will eventually be made available on videotape. But for the moment the original film languishes in the vaults of the British Film Institute; Shaffer retains the script himself.

Peter Shaffer wrote two other teleplays early in his career. Details regarding both are scarce, because scripts are not available. *Balance of Terror* was broadcast by the BBC on 21 November 1957, and appeared in an American version in CBS's *Studio One* on 27 January 1958. Offhand comments by Shaffer, reviews (generally negative in tone) in *The Times* (22 November 1957) and the *New York Times* (28 January 1958) and an interview in the *New York Herald Tribune* offer what little information is available today. The play takes its theme from the international crises of the 1950s, when Soviet and Western intelligence agents vied to give their respective powers the upper hand in the 'balance of terror' (referring to their arsenals of weapons of mass destruction). A British spy and his Whitehall chief (discovered to be a Russian agent) are dual protagonists in this variation on a detective story. The London *Times* acknowledged inventive plotting but considered the characters stilted. When interviewed a few years later about *Balance of Terror*, Shaffer told the *Herald Tribune* that the American television production had been severely weakened by cuts to his script. The result, he stated, was a staging 'boiled down to the lowest common denominator of American television rubbish' (3 January 1960).

Despite his unhappy experience with American commercial television, Shaffer told me that he accepted a commission to write another teleplay for CBS. The play was completed and submitted but never produced or broadcast. Nor is any script apparently available; the sole copy of this untitled television piece – if it still exists – is held in CBS's archives. John Gielgud was intended to play a British professor of English literature who suffers a nervous breakdown after coming to live in New York's Greenwich Village. Shaffer remains uncertain why the play was never produced, and has no copy of it himself. Consequently little definite can be said about it.

The Prodigal Father, Shaffer's first play produced for radio, was broadcast on 14 September 1957 on the BBC's *Saturday Matinee Show*. In 1944, at the age of eighteen, he had written another short radio piece, called *The Murder of Pamphilius Prawn*, but the BBC had rejected it. *The Prodigal Father*, however, was accepted and produced; and a script and a recording of the broadcast are preserved in the BBC's Play Library at Broadcasting House in London. The twenty-seven page radio script, which includes handwritten alterations, inserts, deletions and other notations, translates into 39 minutes 14 seconds of air time. The play's several intertwined themes lend it more than a passing interest: telescoped into a single situation are sharp oppositions leading to generational, familial, cultural and historical conflicts. As with most of Shaffer's early dramatic works, elements drawn from his own life are discernible. Most important of these is the psychic schism created from living in two countries with quite different cultures. As the story begins, a wealthy American named Leander Johnson arrives with his teen-aged son Jed at Glenister Hall outside London. Lady Glenister, the current owner, can no longer afford to maintain the mansion after the financial chaos of the Second World War, and Johnson has come to view the estate for possible purchase. He had ignored his son after separating from the boy's mother, but now, having

21

become rich, he hopes to compensate for his earlier failure by exposing Jed to a 'better' aristocratic life on an English estate.

The 'generation gap' is not to be bridged so easily, however, and Jed wants nothing to do with the fancy and – to him – rigidly formal house favoured by his father. The boy's years in the United States have been lived in a middle-class setting (Shaffer peppers Jed's speech with 'Wow', 'Gee', and 'You're nuts'), so the portraits lining the walls of Glenister Hall evoke his ridicule, not inspiration. He calls the persons in the pictures the 'snottiest, sourpussiest bunch of people'. The costly artifacts in every room make the house seem to him a 'museum – stuffed with high class junk'. Meantime, Lady Glenister and her young niece Lucy epitomise the elegant, stable traditions of the Old World. Trapped in the increasingly expensive commercialism of post-war England, Lady Glenister can no longer maintain her status through title alone. The plight of the once-élite, with their inheritance of elegance, charm and tradition, is contrasted to the raw energy of the United States, where business success often vitiates finer feelings.

Jed and Lucy, the young people who eventually will inherit whatever respective national cultures may emerge, hit it off well during Johnson's examination of the house. The boy explains what makes the United States so special to him. Speaking of Americans Jed says, 'That's what keeps them young. They have the feeling if things don't work out they can tear themselves down and start over just like with the buildings . . . That's why they're always changing things. Changing their homes and their automobiles and their wives and their analysts . . . to make life more . . . well – just More.'

In declarations such as this and similar ones expressed in *Five Finger Exercise*, *Shrivings* and *Equus* Shaffer projects his own split attitude toward America, where he has lived for six months each year for two decades. He explicitly voices such sentiments in interviews, the introductions to his plays and in the revealing Preface to *The Collected Plays* (1982). Shaffer accepts the rough edges in American culture as the price to be paid for American social egalitarianism and business prowess. *The Prodigal Father* concludes with Johnson's acceptance of Jed's preference for American life, and father and son decide to return to the United States and cultivate new lives together. Leander Johnson thus becomes the 'prodigal' who is set on the correct path by his own offspring. Not until *Lettice & Lovage* in 1987 did Shaffer again focus so completely on matters of taste and cultural values.

On a lighter note, in 1963 Shaffer contributed two satirical sketches to the popular British television series *That Was the Week that Was*. The two short pieces – 'But My Dear' and 'The President of France' – followed on the heels of the playwright's initial excursion into comedy, the two one-acters *The Private Ear* and *The Public Eye*, which had been premiered on the London stage a year earlier. Although little more than literary trifles, these television scripts reveal a more biting, ironic side to Shaffer's art, one which did not appear in his stage comedies until *Black Comedy*. 'But My Dear' is constructed on the browbeating of a subordinate civil servant by his superior, centring on possible sexual connotations lying in the subtext of even mundane business correspondence. The boss's polemics against homosexuality add to the facetious portrait of overbearing literalists, always a *bête noire* where Shaffer is concerned. In 'The President of France' a Charles de

Gaulle-like character delivers a sarcastic acceptance speech upon being chosen the Supreme Chief Spokesman of the European Community. The irony of the script now seems more biting than it originally did, inasmuch as Shaffer sets the speech in the year 1990, uncannily close to the year when the European nations will institute a customs union, on the way to even greater economic and political unity. Historical allusions are profuse in this sketch, which centres vaguely on the messianic impulse found among leaders in all times and places. Both sketches demonstrate that satire is one of the weapons in Shaffer's dramatic arsenal, but they are too slender for any profound conclusions to be drawn from them. Fortunately, unlike most of Shaffer's broadcast dramas, the texts of these two minor pieces have been published (in *That Was the Week That Was*, edited by David Frost and Ned Sherrin, 1963).

One further minor sketch deserves mention, a Christmas entertainment (with songs by Stanley Myers) called *The Merry Roosters Panto*. First produced at Wyndham's Theatre, London, on 19 December 1963, this frolic was intended to provide matinee amusement before the evening show, *Oh What a Lovely War!* As directed by Joan Littlewood (also revived by her at The Place in London on 26 December 1969), *The Merry Roosters Panto* proved a modest success with its British audiences, who are more familiar with pantomime than playgoers in other parts of the world. Children are specifically targeted audiences, and Shaffer elicited an energetic response from his youthful spectators. Within a traditional pierrot party framework, Shaffer wrote a contemporary version of the Cinderella fairy tale which featured an astronaut as the prince and a new villain figure called Redsocks. Again, the piece is too slight to permit any broad generalisations, and, without a published script for reference, no close analysis of it is possible.[12]

In my first interviews with Shaffer, during 1980, he showed little inclination to write for commercial television or radio again. His reasons shed light on his creative premises. First is a strong preference for 'live' theatre, centred on a 'congregation' (his term) of author, performer and playgoer. He values the unique emotional and intellectual circuitry created by all three elements during live production. He also believes that human beings are diminished (literally and metaphorically) when their images are 'flashed on a measly little television screen'. Most distasteful for Shaffer are the required scenic units of fifteen minutes, the usual interval between commercial breaks. Moreover, Shaffer insists that, despite its positive attributes, television has conditioned viewers to develop a far shorter attention span than is required for live theatre performances. All the same Shaffer admits that, because television 'is a perfect medium . . . through which to express certain internal experiences', he does not rule out entirely the possibility of ever writing teleplays again.

As for radio, in May 1989 his new one-person radio play *Whom Do I Have the Honour of Addressing?* was broadcast by the BBC. Judi Dench played Angela, the middle-aged Englishwoman who is the sole character in the funny script. The play uses a single setting, Angela's flat in London, and the piece is a monologue. Angela is heard dictating into a tape recorder the recent events of her shocking and unfortunate dealings with Tom Prance, a notorious Hollywood playboy who had taken her to California as private secretary. Conflict on one level arises when the taped narrative is played back, as counterpoint to Angela's words being spoken at the moment. More conflict occurs when Angela righteously attacks Prance's irregular sexual proclivities. Shaffer has stated (in an interview with me in March 1990) that the piece was originally written for Maggie Smith, to give her something to do while she was recuperating from a serious bicycle accident late in 1988. Miss Smith, however, was unable to take part, and Judi Dench agreed to accept the role. Shaffer says he may expand the script into a television or stage drama, but, as performed on air, *Whom Do I Have the Honour of Addressing?* remains simply a radio piece. In any event, Shaffer evidently has not entirely turned his back on broadcast drama, even in the post-*Amadeus* era of his career.[13]

2
Launching a Theatre Career: 'Five Finger Exercise'

Once Peter Shaffer's plays found their way onto the stage, success followed quickly. *Five Finger Exercise*, premiered on 16 July 1958 at the Comedy Theatre in London's West End, attracted handsome reviews in both the British and the American press. The magazine *Stage and Television Today* considered *Five Finger Exercise* 'the best play in the West End in a long time'; *Punch* noted that 'Shaffer has something to say and says it skilfully'. *The Times* commented prophetically that 'Mr Shaffer may easily become a master of the theatre', while the *Illustrated London News* announced, 'Shaffer writes with a feeling for phrase demonstrated by few recent playwrights.' The first London production ran for 610 performances – an unusually long run for a serious drama in the West End.

Part of the initial impact of *Five Finger Exercise* stemmed from the strong production it received. Considering that Shaffer was little known at the time, the company responsible for staging the play, H. M. Tennent, took a considerable commercial risk in accepting it for the West End, yet nothing was held back. John Gielgud was engaged to direct veteran actor Roland Culver and talented newcomers Brian Bedford, Michael Bryant and Juliet Mills, and with one change (Jessica Tandy replaced Adrianne Allen as Louise) the same cast opened in New York City the following year (2 December) at the Music Box Theatre. The play was an even greater critical success in America than in London. The dean of New York critics, Brooks Atkinson of the *New York Times*, termed it a 'gem of civilized theatre', and Harold Clurman considered the drama an advance for British theatre. *Five Finger Exercise* earned numerous awards, including Best Play by a New Playwright for the 1958–9 season (London newspaper critics' award) and Best Foreign Play in the 1959–60 New York theatre season.

In line with the conservative approach of Shaffer's broadcast dramas, *Five Finger Exercise* is a naturalistic play, and does not use the presentational modes adopted for such later works as *The Royal Hunt of the Sun*, *Equus*, *Amadeus* and *Yonadab*. The action takes place on a multiple set depicting several rooms of the Harringtons' '*week-end cottage in Suffolk*'. Within the drawing-room context (which Shaffer's stage directions describe with novelistic thoroughness) the five characters in the drama interrelate according to meticulously defined motivations. Scenes proceed in chronological order; dialogue, not flashback, fills in details from the past. All in all, it is a talky play, but one in which Shaffer's strong dramatic sense makes listening worthwhile. Shaffer's talent for fashioning character is strongly in evidence. All five characters are given full psychological co-ordinates. Each person's quirks and wants are painstakingly developed, and are rounded out with characteristics which are neither strengths or weaknesses but simply make the character what he or she is. As a result, the audience always understands why characters behave as they do. The well-made-play format of *Five Finger Exercise* reveals little technical daring, but the play is finely shaped, exemplifying representational theatre at its most effective. Shaffer offers no apologies for the style used, saying, 'I feel I did crafted work in my first piece. It said what I wanted it to say, and it possessed a shape which made it play easily and finally accumulated its power. This quality of *shape* is very important to me.'[1]

Thematically, *Five Finger Exercise* reflects its 1950s heritage as filtered through the youthful idealism of the playwright. The Second World War was still high in the collective consciousness of Western Europe at the time. Compounding the war's horrors were the revelations then surfacing about the Holocaust. It was time to turn one's back on the agony, and Europeans were eager to return to peacetime activities. In Great Britain that meant taking up anew the pre-war goal of making money. A new breed of outspoken critics of England's stratified society began to politicise the theatre, however. Young and radical, they argued that Britain should not return to 'business as usual' in a changed post-Empire world. Shaffer sympathised with their altruistic stance, and incorporated in *Five Finger Exercise* an issue also examined, with more acerbity, by John Osborne and the other 'Angry Young Men': old perspectives – social, economic, philosophical – needed to give way to a fresh approach. Stanley Harrington is Shaffer's specimen of English's old guard, as is Colonel Redfern in Osborne's *Look Back in Anger*.

Shaffer's choice of title is apt. A 'five-finger exercise' is a means for training a pianist in keyboard technique. All five fingers must play an equal part to avoid disharmony. In comparable fashion, *Five Finger Exercise* demonstrates how compulsive acts by one member of a family can disrupt the delicate balance of the whole. Five characters make up the cast, and each person's story is woven into an integrated design to expose everyone's innermost desires and vulnerabilities. At the start of the play, four members of the Harrington family – parents Stanley and Louise, and offspring Clive and Pamela – are shown functioning together in an uneasy alliance. Each gives and receives from the others in a system acceded to by all. As a consequence, the family functions harmoniously even if uneasily. In the opening scenes, Shaffer introduces his characters, gradually moving them into a collision course that threatens discord. The play moves toward a climax when, as in his detective novels, Shaffer peels away the characters' façades to reveal the hidden motives driving the action. The arrival on the scene of a fifth person, the handsome German tutor Walter Langer, is what jeopardises the precarious relationships among the Harringtons. Shaffer uses Langer in important ways in the plot. On the one hand, Walter's gentle uprightness elicits confidence – and confidences – from the Harringtons. Recent scholarship suggests that family members confess their deceptions and self-deceptions because of their guest's magnetic personality.[2] But more than psychological hand-holding is involved. Each family member expects something specific from the young foreigner – not spiritual expiation expressed on the surface, but some sort of sexual fulfilment, whether real or fantasised. When Walter is unwilling to respond to those expectations, only his expulsion allows the family to regain its delicate

equilibrium. Sexual dynamics insidiously subvert the characters' best intentions.

Yet purging Walter from their midst cannot alone rid
the Harringtons of the fundamental impasse which sty-
mies them. He simply stumbles into a corrosive family
situation at the wrong moment, becoming a casualty in the
Harringtons' guerrilla war. Clive warns Walter early
against becoming enamoured of his family, insisting that
'sooner or later you will be used . . . I know this family,
let me tell you' (p.33). The fate of each character depends
on the others in the manner of a psychological geodesic
dome: an abrupt shift in any one vector will bring the
whole crashing down.

Clive is the prize vigorously fought over by his mother
and father. A college student, he stands on the threshold
of adulthood, midway through his rites of passage. Shaffer
portrays him struggling to determine fundamental choices
about his life and career. He is drawn towards a career in
writing and the fine arts, and on the personal level has
homosexual inclinations. As a pawn of his mother's and
father's conflicting ambitions for him, he is challenged on
all sides. Each parent insists on defining Clive's life
course, in the process subjecting him to intense psychological pressure. Most intimidating to Clive is his businessman father, Stanley, whose philistine approach to life is in
direct conflict with Louise's dilettantism. In the Preface to
the *Collected Plays*, Shaffer acknowledges parallels between his own upbringing and that of Clive. Like Clive he
found himself under pressure to accept parental standards, in particular those of the father. In Shaffer's words,
'as an adolescent I had bought the lie, assiduously circu-
lated by the world I was born into, that business is reality
and art pretence . . . A frustrated fellow in my twenties, I
went on believing that what I enjoyed doing – writing –

was frivolous, and what bored me completely – com-
merce – was serious' (p.viii). But Shaffer cautions against
interpreting everything about Clive as autobiographical.
The sole direct link was, in Shaffer's words, 'the tension
between my mother and father in which I was involved'.[3]

The Apollonian and Dionysian antithesis that dominates
Shaffer's later dramas receives its initial presentation
in *Five Finger Exercise*. Here Stanley's pragmatism
manifests the Apollonian emphasis on order and efficiency;
Langer too, we shall see, pursues the Apollonian path
based on order. Harrington is a team player who 'plays
the game' dictated by society in order to attain his
worldly objectives. Louise follows her imagination and
creative impulses in typical Dionysian fashion, as does
Clive. Neither clear-cut villains nor saints, both parents
appear as recognisable modern human beings. Husband
and father, Stanley nominally heads the household.
Emerging from a middle-class background, he became a
self-made man who now leads a profitable company that
manufactures cut-rate office furniture. He wholeheartedly
embraces the notion of capitalistic materialism. For him,
money and the power it brings are the major goals in life.
All else – courtesy, culture, contemplation – is expend-
able window-dressing. Stanley states his position bluntly
to Louise: 'Don't ever be so stupid as to look down on
money. It's the one thing that counts in the end' (p.25).
Money alone carries weight. Even Stanley's interest in
sports is used to cultivate business contacts, he slyly
confesses to his son.

Harrington expresses one further aim in his life: to have
his only son follow in his footsteps. Such a possibility
seems less likely as the lad grows up, and Stanley clearly is
worried. When Clive returns home from Cambridge for
the summer holidays, Stanley learns that his son's univers-

ity routine involves writing poetry and theatre reviews. Having not needed a university degree himself for success, Stanley considers Clive's activities a squandering of time and energy. Gruffly, he badgers his son, 'And this is the most useful thing you can find to do with your time?' (p.9). Stanley takes every occasion to convert his son to a more practical career track. Sometimes cajoling, sometimes threatening, he preaches a gospel of hard work and accumulation of wealth. Impatient with other interests, he insists, 'All this culture stuff's very fine for those who can afford it . . . but it's not going to earn you the price of sausage outside this front door' (p.10). Neither more nor less than many fathers, Harrington wants to make his son in his own image.

Nor does Stanley hide his disdain for Clive's 'cultured' friends at university, considering them useless parasites on English society. Especially objectionable are the unmasculine traits he sees in 'artistic people', and he often reminds Clive how crucial appearances are in business for making the 'right' impression. His deepest worry is that Clive could be demasculinised by his 'arty' college chums and maybe drawn into homosexuality. In Stanley, Shaffer creates a well-intentioned but blinkered bigot who continually berates Clive for keeping company with the 'wrong crowd': 'I mayn't be much in the way of education, but I know this: if you can't stand on your own two feet you don't amount to anything. And not one of that pansy set of spongers you're going around with will ever help you do that . . . I've seen them. Arty-tarty boys. They think it's clever going round Chelsea and places like that giggling and drinking and talking dirty, wearing Bohemian clothes. Tight trousers' (p.10). Connected to his disdain for unmanly men is Stanley's sensitivity to his own lower-middle-class roots. He is a precursor of Frank Strang in

33

Equus, another husband and father made to feel inferior
and inadequate by a wife born into a higher class. In an
illogical but human reaction, Stanley defends his social
status by attacking another social group. Weary of being
browbeaten by Louise, he gleefully attacks Clive's effete
friends: 'Who gave them the right to look down on other
people, that's what I want to know, just because they
don't know about the [*affected voice*] *operah* and the
ballay and the *dramah*?' (p.10). Yet he understands that
the true enemy is his wife, who encourages Clive in all his
artistic experiments. She is a formidable antogonist,
undercutting her husband at every opportunity with con-
descending remarks. When he complains that Clive has
openly criticised the design of the furniture his firm
makes, she retorts, 'Just because *you've* got no taste, it
doesn't mean we all have to follow suit' (p.22). The battle
lines between Louise and Stanley are clearly drawn.

A true dilettante, Louise is a compelling figure in her
own right. She is the product of a modest but refined
family upbringing. Her father was a professor and her
mother allegedly an aristocratic Frenchwoman immersed
in the arts and humanitarian causes. However, her
father's inept management of domestic and commercial
finances brought the family to grief. Thus, when Louise
grew to marriageable age, she had few alternatives.
Raised with cultured tastes and art objects around her, she
could not settle for a life of anything less. A cultivated
young woman without independent means might logically
consider marrying a rising businessman, and to Louise's
parents Stanley seemed a suitable 'catch'. There was
hesitation about the marriage at first, because of their
different backgrounds: in Louise's words, 'socially the
thing was far from ideal' (p.28). But eventually her
parents dismissed any reservations because 'They wanted

me to have all the comforts they couldn't give me themselves' (p. 28).

Marrying Stanley answered Louise's primary needs and allowed her to pursue a life of genteel culture. Ironically, her match with Stanley was strictly a business arrangement whereby Stanley 'bought' an upper-class trophy to display, and Louise 'contracted' for a life secure in material goods. She complains openly about her sacrifice in marrying Stanley, saying to Walter, 'these last few years have been intolerable' (p. 29). She insists that she has stayed with her husband for the children's sake: 'At least I could see that *they* weren't stifled too'. Although attractive and refined, she has grown into a fullblown harridan, and Stanley cultivates a separate life for himself in order to escape the inhospitable atmosphere at home. Domestic matters are left wholly to Louise, who runs the home with an iron fist. Shaffer's stage directions describing the Harrington residence emphasise that its decor reflects *Louise's* tastes: the *'well furnished living room . . . almost aggressively expresses* MRS HARRINGTON'S *personality'*. She influences Clive to adopt her artistic interests. Increasingly the object of heated contention in the Harrington home, Clive is held psychological hostage by both parents, each of whom is intent on determining how he will turn out. The contest for his loyalty triggers numberless skirmishes between Louise and Stanley, which in turn generates unrelieved tension in the home. Still, the family 'glue' appears to hold, at least until a powerful centrifugal force is added.

Shaffer has made Louise as a fully rounded character. Her aggressiveness and breezy manner mask a deep-seated fear of losing what she considers her proper place in the social order, her identity. She feels cut off from cultivated persons who could reinforce her social esteem.

Harrington's commercial interests and acquaintances provide her no outlets, nor does Stanley possess the debonair personality she requires in order to shine. That unanswered need for a 'civilised' companion helps explain why Louise hires the handsome twenty-two-year-old Langer as a tutor for Pamela. Whenever a conversation moves towards an intellectual or artistic topic, she taunts Stanley with, 'Of course I don't expect *you* to understand.' Walter is a counterweight to Stanley's leaden philistinism.

Meanwhile Langer follows his own odyssey. He is guilt-ridden over Germany's part in the Second World War. More particularly, he is mortified by his own parents' willing acquiescence in Hitler's grandiose plans – including the Final Solution of the Jewish 'problem'. In comparing English and the German national traits, Langer underscores his pro-English bias: 'Here in England most people *want* to do what's good. Where I was born this is not true. They want only power . . . They are a people that is enraged by equality.' England for Walter, 'is Paradise' (p. 30). He is determined to obtain British citizenship and once and for all turn his back on his German heritage. For that reason, he is extremely careful not to jeopardise his chances to gain recommendations from the Harringtons, his employers. He explains to Clive, 'So you see, I do know what it is to have a family. And what I look for . . . [*in strange tone.*] A house where now and then good spirits can sit on the roof.' Clive instantly replies, 'And you think you've found it here? Do you? . . . You're fooling yourself every minute' (p. 53). Yet Walter's compulsion is so strong that, despite all his precautions, he is caught in the family's infighting, to end up their victim.

Shaffer effectively develops the domestic snarling among the Harringtons during the opening scenes. His

plot inventiveness comes to the fore with the introduction
of the fifth character in the 'five finger' pattern. As
outsider, Walter is called upon to serve as buffer and
mediator during the frequent family skirmishes. As the
plot progresses, he is drawn increasingly into the family's
domestic problems. Gradually, three of the Harringtons – Louise, Pamela and Clive – reach out to possess
Walter, all in their own way and for their own reasons.
Rock-solid in character, he responds forthrightly and
candidly to each. But he also alienates each by rejecting
their intimate overtures. Dramatic interest is heightened
as three Harringtons subtly respond to a sexual magnetism
in Walter of which he himself seems unaware.

Pamela's relationship with Walter is the simplest. A
sensitive adolescent of fourteen, she sympathises with him
upon hearing his sad life. Moreover, in Shaffer's short but
lively portrait she is starting to sense her femininity and feel
a physical attraction to boys. Through his French lessons,
she becomes progressively close to Walter, even touching
him in innocent friendliness. Shaffer writes into Pamela a
brightness and sense of humour not seen in the other
Harringtons. She enjoys teasing, and jokingly suggests
that Walter should cultivate a more romantic appearance:
'You should wear a high collar. And one of those floppy
ties. Then you'd look like Metternich or someone. And
wear your hair very sleek and romantic. [*She smooths his
hair*.] Like this . . .' (p. 15). Throughout the early scenes
she greatly admires Walter. At one point she gushes,
'He's so fresh! Fresh and beautiful' (p. 49). But she lacks
emotional maturity, and cannot handle the situation when
the stirrings of affection for Langer take hold. When he
fails to respond to her innocent overtures she becomes
noticeably moody. Her sulking eventually provides Louise
with the pretext for dismissing him. Though the most

innocent of the Harringtons in her dealings with Walter, even Pamela manipulates others, sometimes tragically. Nor does she come to Walter's defence at the end of the play, further confirming Clive's remark about the family's destructiveness.

Meanwhile Louise's admiration of Walter's cultured background expands into physical desire. Their relationship begins innocently, Walter remaining a thoughtful listener to her complaints about Stanley. She also enjoys Walter's unrestrained idolisation of the Harrington home: 'If you had seen what I have, you would know why I call it Paradise' (p. 31). Walter's obvious suffering over his German background also brings out Louise's consoling instincts. He in turn '*impulsively . . . bends and kisses her hands*' in gratitude for her understanding, inducing Louise to take his head in her hands, and to draw him close. Innocent physical moments such as this stimulate Louise's romantic fantasising over a man young enough to be her son.

By the end of Act I, Louise believes herself in love with Walter. She begins making overtures to him, telling him, 'You know, last night held the most beautiful moments I've known for many years. I felt – well, that you and I could have a really warm friendship. Even with the difference . . . I mean in – in our ages' (p. 54). She is, however, irremediably hardened against him when, unaware of her growing physical interest in him, he indicates that he feels for her as for a surrogate mother: 'Mrs Harrington, forgive me for asking this, but do you think it's possible for someone to find a new mother?' (p. 55). Stunned and humiliated, she soon finds an excuse – his alleged negative effect on Pamela – to fire him.

Clive is the third member of the family to relate disastrously with Langer. Shaffer attains the highest level of complexity and interest in the Clive and Walter axis:

theirs is the sole instance in which an intellectual bond is formed. This continuous pressure applied to Clive by both parents has seriously eroded his self-confidence. Near the close of the first act Clive explodes, accusing his father of not understanding children. His half-drunken criticism of Stanley offers a perspective on his reaction to the family's squabbles: 'But *you* don't even know the right way to treat a child. Because a child is private and important and *itself*. Not an extension of you, any more than I am . . . I am myself. Myself. Myself. You think of me only as what I might become. What I might make of myself. But I am myself now . . .' (pp.37–8). Clive is determined not to be a copy of either parent but to become his own person. Walter meantime serves as a sympathetic sounding-board for Clive because of what they have in common. Both young men are ready to launch their adult lives, and both passionately strive to sustain personal goals despite outside social and economic impositions. Walter is someone with whom Clive can talk candidly, and in his mind Clive constructs strong links between them.

Often in *Five Finger Exercise* Clive begins to speak confessionally to Walter as a confident, expressing feelings half-buried in guilt and embarrassment. Surprisingly, it turns out, Clive resents his mother nearly as much as he does his father. Mockingly, he parodies her for Walter: 'If we can't have a château in Brittany, then we *can* have a country place in Suffolk, which is almost as desolate but rather more convenient. If we can't install scholars in our library, because we haven't got a library, since nobody reads in our house, why, then, the least we can do is get in a dear gentle tutor for the girl. Someone with tone, of course . . . You see, we're specialists in delicacy' (p. 32). Mentally, the two are well-matched, and they seemingly should relate easily with one another.

But crucial to Clive's individuality is his sexuality. And central to his sexuality is incipient homosexuality. Clive's attraction toward Langer steadily grows, and with a few drinks in him Clive runs his fingers through Walter's hair. Mistakenly sensing more kinship than actually exists between them, Clive claims to understand Walter's situation: 'You think I don't know how lonely you were before you came here. You're wrong, I can smell your loneliness . . .' (p. 34). Suddenly, following his innermost instincts, Clive begs Walter to run off with him. In a barely disguised homosexual proposal he urges, 'Come away with me . . . If you came away with me, it would be for my sake – not yours. I need a friend so badly'. Apollonian in his dedication to rules and self-control, Walter demurs, claiming that his foremost obligation is to Louise, who hired him. His rebuff causes a serious crisis, because, beside the physical attraction he feels for the German, Clive also experiences jealousy. Earlier, upon entering the room without warning, he saw Louise innocently embracing Walter. He now is crushed by the rejection and angered by Louise's display of affection toward the tutor. The combination of emotion overcomes Clive's Dionysian soul. In the stunning scene which closes the first act, he retaliates. Drunkenly he blurts out to Stanley a distorted version of the episode: 'There on the sofa. I saw them. I came in and there they were. The light was turned down. They were kissing. *Kissing!* She was half undressed, and he was kissing her, on the mouth. On the breasts. Kissing . . .' (p. 39). Walter's hopes of remaining in the Harrington house are dashed. For the third time he has innocently turned down affection from one of the Harringtons. Again he fails to mesh with other 'fingers' making up that family.

Stanley is the only Harrington who does not seek

anything from Walter. All the same, once Louise has asked him to dismiss the tutor, Stanley takes the opportunity to quiz Walter about his relationship to Clive. It is obvious from their conversation that Stanley does not consider himself in any way responsible for his son's alienation from the family. He insists, 'I'll tell you why he drinks. So he can get over being with me. Have you noticed how this family of mine never get together in this house?' (p. 62). Tentatively, Walter risks offending by responding directly to Stanley's demand for an opinion: 'I think he feels you do not love him, but still are expecting him to love you . . . You see, in front of you he must always justify his life' (p. 52). Walter's reply is not what Stanley wants to hear, since he is looking for someone else to blame for his failure to relate with his son. His chance comes soon after, when he overhears Walter offering Clive some disquieting advice.

Much of Clive's difficulty in formulating a secure personal identity involves sexual confusion. In a crucial scene leading to the play's climax, Walter finally risks his secure fence-sitting stance and makes an all-out effort to help Clive. Having failed to make Stanley listen, Walter wants all the more to clarify matters for Clive, suggesting that 'You must try to forgive your parents for being average and wrong when you worshipped them once.' To allay Clive's concern about sex, Langer expounds on its limitation: 'Do you think sex will change you? Put you into a different world, where everything will mean more to you? . . . Sex by itself is nothing, believe me. Just like breathing – only important when it goes wrong' (p. 64). But Walter's reasonable words at first fail to inspire Clive. Only drastic action will give him a chance to discover his own identity. Now deeply involved in his friend's situation, Walter urges Clive to get on with his life: 'break the glass! Get out of the coffin! Jump up and begin yourself. Make up your own time without one minute when you don't care who you are . . . But you must go away from here' (pp. 65–6). This time Clive is convinced, and agrees to leave home with its suffocating influences.

Clive thus finds an answer for his dilemma. But Walter's life will be ruined. When he overhears Walter encouraging Clive to leave home to create a separate life, Stanley sees his authority in the family challenged. His inflexible male pride is bruised, and he turns on the hapless German in self-righteous fury. Using self-justifying rationalisation, he accuses Walter of homosexual encounters with Clive – of turning his 'son into a sissy'. Additionally, he charges Langer of usurping parental control over Clive: 'He's a mess, that's what he is. And it's your fault . . . *Yours.* You, the arty boys. It's you who've taken him . . . [*Hurling the names as if they were insults.*] Shakespeare! Beethoven! . . . All the time, till I can't touch him . . . What gave you the right to steal my boy?' (p. 66). Stanley's *coup de grâce* is to dismiss Walter on the spot, claiming that he has unsettled Pamela. Walter denies the charge but is silenced when Stanley adds a second motive for the dismissal: Clive's report that Walter has been carrying on with Louise. Stanley smugly exiles the German from his home and simultaneously destroys the tutor's dreams of making a new life in England. Clive's warning that the Harringtons would eventually ruin Walter is confirmed. Horror-struck by betrayal on every side – by Louise, Pamela, Stanley and even Clive – Walter turns desperate and attempts suicide at the end of the play.

No single theme dominates Shaffer's sombre drama. Much like a young novelist's first book, *Five Finger Exercise* builds on a youth 'finding himself' amid a myriad

42

of conflicting influences Clive, however, is no stock figure in a conventional rites-of-passage design. Shaffer creates him with multiple dimensions to reveal someone whose interaction with others rings true. Each member of the Harrington clan is a unique persona characterised by specific wants and motivations. Non-stop action begins when the dramatist turns loose the four Harringtons, effecting a grand mosaic of conflicting wills. The discrete lives function – mesh – together until the outside catalyst, Walter Langer, disrupts the family concord. Walter's presence precipitates the exposure of the others' individual desires. As a result, the plot revolves to show a series of doomed relationships – marital dissonance, incipient love (heterosexual and homosexual), generational crisis and betrayal of friendship. Ironically, the rites-of-passage element – Clive's will to determine his own life path – ends up being simply one strand amid a range of conflicting wants. The resulting unfulfilled needs lead to the sense of universal desolation later also felt in *Royal Hunt*, *Equus* and *Yonadab*.[4] Because of Shaffer's thoroughly etched characterisations and his carefully synchronised plot threads, *Five Finger Exercise* furnishes a portrait of contemporary life not easily forgotten.

3
Four One-Act Comedies and 'Shrivings'

When *Five Finger Exercise* brought him international attention in 1958, Peter Shaffer was a young man of thirty-two, experimenting with prose fiction along with drama. During the twelve-year period between *Five Finger Exercise* and *The Battle of Shrivings*, he devoted all his creative energies to drama, working with a variety of formats and techniques. Among the successes from this productive time were London and Broadway productions of four one-act comedies, a major film script (*Lord of the Flies*, 1963, co-authored with Peter Brook), skits and revues for stage and television (*The Merry Roosters' Panto* and *That Was the Week that Was*, both 1963, and a monumental dramatic epic (*The Royal Hunt of the Sun*, 1964). Closing this period in his career, a new full-length drama, *The Battle of Shrivings* (1970), faltered in London after a short run. That failure remains painful to the playwright to this day. Yet its deficiencies alerted Shaffer to problematic elements in his writing, notably a tendency to slip into overheated language when dealing with serious themes.

Midway between *Five Finger Exercise* and *The Battle of Shrivings* came *The Royal Hunt of the Sun*, perhaps the most bold and inventive endeavour of Shaffer's career. Its incorporation of inspired (and audacious) theatrical visualisations attracted intense attention from playgoers and critics alike. Moreover, the drama's cluster of provocative themes, ranging from bankrupt religion to myopic national chauvinism, suggested a writer of daring. Although not all the dramatic elements interact convincingly in this hybrid play, for its array of extraordinary dramatic qualities *Royal Hunt* warrants a chapter of its own (Ch. 4). Meanwhile, *The Battle of Shrivings* (or *Shrivings*, as revised) and the four one-acters comprise an identifiable unit of technical experimentation and development. These pieces may usefully be considered together as we chart the development of Shaffer's craft in the earlier years of his career.

Each of his one-acters from the 1960s adds to the picture we have of Shaffer's emerging stagecraft. Taken together, they represent a proving ground for themes, techniques and characters that appear in the later dramas. Of the four plays, *Black Comedy* and *The Public Eye* are generally considered outstanding, *The Private Ear* technically solid but dated, and *White Liars* laboured and leaden.[1] These works have a number of characteristics in common. All except *Black Comedy* have three-person casts of two men and a woman. Shaffer's propensity for punning and wordplay is evident in the titles of all his comedies, including the more recent *Lettice & Lovage*. Moreover, aside from *Lettice & Lovage*, which is a

45

full-length play, Shaffer's comedies treat different aspects of love. Despite these common attributes, however, the four one-act comedies exhibit more differences than similarities in texture and pacing.

The two earliest comedies, *The Private Ear* and *The Public Eye*, were premiered as a double bill on 10 May 1962 at London's Globe Theatre. Late the following year, the plays received a first staging in New York at the former Morosco Theatre. Of the two works, *The Private Ear* has a more conventional structure and is therefore more predictable. The plot is standard fare in comedy, involving the vicissitudes of first love. Bob, a clumsy bachelor living in modern London, wants to impress Doreen, a girl he met at a symphony concert. Their first 'date' is for dinner at his flat. His gaucheness, however, loses her to his friend Ted, who is more experienced with girls. Shaffer's story of adolescent love does not conclude with Bob's becoming more accomplished in amorous relationships. In fact he gains painful confirmation of his ineptness in the ritual of courtship. Shaffer ends the smoothly crafted comedy with a bittersweet twist befitting the love combat between Bob and Ted for Doreen.

In London, Doreen was played by Maggie Smith, then at the outset of an illustrious stage and film career. Douglas Livingstone played Ted, and Terry Scully was Bob. Directing both in England and later in the United States was Peter Wood. On Broadway the performers were Geraldine McEwen (Doreen), Brian Bedford (Bob), and Barry Foster (Ted). Critical response to the double bill began as moderately positive, with public enthusiasm increasing during the London run. Each play in the double bill had its advocates. Laudatory reviews of *The Private Ear* were written by W. A. Darlington (*Daily Telegraph*, 11 May 1962), Milton Shulman (*Evening Standard*, 11

May 1962) and J. C. Trewin (*Illustrated London News*, 26
May 1962).[2] American critics touted both plays. Martin
Gottfried's review in *Women's Wear Daily* (10 October
1963) singled out *The Private Ear* as particularly impressive – a view shared by Henry Hewes in the *Saturday
Review* (26 October 1963) and by George Oppenheimer in
the Long Island *Newsday* (10 October 1963). Commentators generally praised the well-defined comic characters
and situations. In a few cases they complained about
contrived cuteness in both pieces.[3]

Looking back at *The Private Ear* today, one is aware of
how profoundly public morality has changed since the
work was written, and of how innocent Shaffer's depiction
of first love is in this play. Also evident is his firm control
of dramatic characterisation. He loses no time in contrasting the two young men. Ted, older and more worldly,
enters Bob's flat to help him prepare dinner for Doreen.
The opening dialogue contrasts Ted's suavity with Bob's
inexperience. Ted challenges his friend: 'What the hell
have you been up to while I've been doing your shopping?
Dreaming, I suppose, as usual . . . You're marvellous!
The most important night of your life, and you can't even
get yourself dressed. All you can do is listen to bloody
music' (pp. 80–1). Shaffer quickly establishes the preda-
tory nature of Ted, who eggs on Bob to use the evening
for amorous – that is, sexual – purposes.

TED. . . . You're not going to let me down tonight, are
     you?
BOB. What do you mean?
TED. You know what you're going to do this evening?
     I mean, you know what I'm expecting you to do,
     don't you?
BOB. Look, Ted, it's not that way at all.

TED. . . . Well then, I'm wasting my time here,
   aren't I?   (p. 81)

Predictably, Bob botches the dinner despite Ted's careful
promptings. When she arrives, Doreen turns out scarcely
less nervous than Bob, and the evening becomes increasingly awkward when no topic inspires sustained conversation. Until Ted enters, that is. Turning on all his charm,
the worldly Ted soon senses that Doreen is drawn to him
rather than to his clumsy friend. Far from being the
rarefied creature Bob imagined, Doreen proves a typical
young girl. Bob's intellectual tastes, meanwhile, epito-
mised by his passion for classical music, alienate him from
Doreen. The musical bond he thought existed between
them does not exist. Though they had met at a classical-
music concert, Doreen eventually admits that she was
given the ticket and had thoroughly disliked the music.

   As the three dine together, Bob makes no headway at
all with the girl. Doreen and Ted, however, strike it off
marvellously. Bob, a non-drinker, makes this evening an
exception, gradually fading into drunken sulkiness. When
the frustrated wooer retreats to the kitchen to make
coffee, Ted and Doreen dance provocatively to the pop
music that Ted plays on the record-player. Inspired by the
wine, the usually mild-mannered Bob accuses Ted of
betraying him. Ted leaves angrily, providing Bob with one
last chance to win Doreen for himself. Despite Doreen's
obvious lack of interest in him (or in classical music), Bob
in desperation choreographs what for him is a romantic
moment: he plays lush love arias and duets from Puccini's
opera *Madame Butterfly* on the record-player. Doreen
surprisingly finds herself enjoying the sweet arias, and,
observing that fact, Bob clumsily makes his move. Seeing
Bob's amorous intentions and feeling sorry for him,

Doreen permits him to kiss her lightly. But, when his actions become more earnest, she slaps him. Bob's evening is ruined, his hopes of succeeding with the rituals of courtship more impossible than ever. Once Doreen has left, the play concludes with Bob, totally distraught, destroying his recording of *Madame Butterfly*.

Although a bittersweet flavour is prominent in retelling the plot, witty dialogue and many comical situations claim the viewer's attention in performance. Shaffer's strengths with comedy lie in several quarters. His characterisations are effectively delineated for maximum contrast, permitting the antagonists to play off one another. Ted is depicted as worldly wise where girls are concerned. He holds no illusions regarding the dynamics of a male–female relationship, and sex is his ultimate goal in each encounter. Bob is portrayed as inexperienced and insecure with girls. His *naïveté* offers unending occasions for laughter once both men begin vying for the same girl. Ted retorts cynically when Bob worries that Doreen might not keep their date:

BOB.   Do you think she's not coming?
TED.   Of course she's coming, It's a free dinner, isn't
    it? (p. 82)

The comedy associated with Doreen derives from other sources. Far from being the idyllic girl of taste that Bob believes her to be, Doreen is a simple girl with mundane interests – such as boys and future marital security. Bob thinks on a more cerebral plane, and mistakenly treats Doreen as an equal, baffling her with his lofty talk. The resulting misunderstandings prompt continuous laughter. When Doreen remarks on Bob's array of recordings, for example, he eagerly responds by offering to play her favourite:

> BOB. . . . which *Brandenburg* would you like? Or maybe you'd prefer the *Goldbergs*? Or the *Musical Offering*?
> DOREEN. [*who has never heard of any of these*]. You choose. (p. 92)

Little physical action occurs in *The Private Ear*, requiring that clever lines sustain the play's interest. None the less, within the limited scope of the plot, Shaffer polishes a number of devices that he often exploits in his later works. Background music, for instance, is skilfully integrated into the plots of several of Shaffer's dramas. The playing of music contributes to the atmosphere desired, as in *The Royal Hunt of the Sun* and *Yonadab*. Shaffer also associates particular types of music with characters to denote their social tastes. Classical compositions are performed on the piano in *Five Finger Exercise* to define Walter's civilised sensibility, while the mundane background of Tom and Frank in *White Liars* is mirrored by their rock music. Of course, music may itself be the centre of a drama, as in the enormously popular *Amadeus*, where Mozart's music plays a key role in the plot. In *The Private Ear* Shaffer contrasts Ted and Bob through their divergent musical preferences: Bob is fanatical about classical music, while Ted selects romantic pop to accompany his amorous pursuits. Ted wins Doreen's affections with his popular dance music, while Bob makes no romantic progress using serious music – a fact confirming Doreen's unexceptional cultural taste. Excerpts from the opera *Madame Butterfly* succeed in emphasising the theme of romantic love gone awry.[4] Throughout the last scene of the play the opera plays loudly on Bob's record-player as he makes one final try to win Doreen. For six minutes the recording blares and no word is spoken; tension grows while Doreen and Bob sit on his bed listening. All the while, Bob sidles nearer his beloved, preparing to kiss her when the music swells to a passionate climax. This interval provides a rich opportunity for comic mimed action, a technique that Shaffer also exploits brilliantly in *Black Comedy*.

From the technical perspective, the most innovative staging occurs during the eating episode. Shaffer's intentions are two: to show that Ted and Doreen are hitting it off well, and to magnify Bob's loss of control of the situation – and of himself – at the dinner table. Shaffer achieves his aims by integrating freeze action, voice-over and symbolic lighting. At the same time he underscores Bob's attempt to numb his humiliation through alcohol:

TED.   [*Smiling*]. Come on. Drink up before it gets cold. *All three lift their spoons. They freeze. The lights go down.* BOB *alone is visible sitting in a spot.*
. . .
The dialogue becomes a high-pitched gabble as the tape is deliberately speeded up.
BOB *puts down his spoon and drinks off an entire glass of wine, quickly. He picks up his spoon again, and freezes.*   (p. 94)

Audiences will recognise the basic 'rite of passage' running through *The Private Ear*. Shaffer has admitted that Bob, like Clive Harrington in *Five Finger Exercise*, has autobiographical overtones. Here, Bob's innocence in matters of the heart triggers the action. If audiences

51

sympathise with anyone in the work, it probably is with Bob and his frustrating plight. None the less, it is not always easy to relate to him. An open conflict of characters arises from the juxtaposition of Ted's bullying tactics and Bob's altruistic sensitivity. Though his ethical values are in theory the most appealing, Bob remains too sentimentalised. His utter helplessness borders on the farcical. Neither Ted nor Doreen has any positive qualities either. Each evidences a familiar personality type, but neither displays attributes likely to endear them to us. Ted's cynical manipulation of others is ruthless and overtly sexist by the standards of any era. Doreen shows little intelligence, imagination or individuality. The comedy as a consequence is left without a character whom playgoers can readily approve, thus depriving the piece of ethical moorings. What the comical situations and clever dialogue of *The Private Ear* confirm, however, is that Shaffer's dramatic range includes finely honed comedy as well as serious domestic drama.

The title of *The Public Eye* complements that of *The Private Ear*, with which it was originally paired. Whereas *The Private Ear* centres on courtship among fledgling lovers, *The Public Eye* takes itself less seriously while treating the marital difficulties of a married couple. A third character in the plot, the private detective Julian Cristoforou, adds spontaneous mischief as the mainspring in the story. Hired by a stuffy, middle-aged accountant who suspects his young wife of infidelity, Cristoforou clears up the misunderstandings that separate the couple. Unlike *The Private Ear*, this one-acter exudes genial humour and concludes with light-hearted laughter.

Maggie Smith received strong London reviews as the young wife Belinda, a role taken by Geraldine McEwan in the United States. Kenneth Williams portrayed the

detective in London (Barry Foster, in America), while
Richard Pearson first created the part of the jealous
husband Charles (Moray Watson, in New York). Most
reviewers preferred the light-spirited *Public Eye* to the
more cynical *Private Ear*. Among those who praised it
most energetically were Harold Hobson (*Christian Science
Monitor*, 12 May 1962), Kenneth Tynan (*Observer*, 13
May 1962), Allan Lewis (*Sunday Herald*, 27 October
1963), John McCarten (*New Yorker*, 19 October 1963)
and Howard Taubman (*New York Theatre Critics' Reviews*, 10 October 1963). Sophisticated wit and pervasive
good humour were given as the play's strongest attributes
by reviewers. The key to the good spirits of the piece lies
with Shaffer's fresh characters, who emerge remarkably
well-delineated even in such a short work.[5]

The freest spirit in the play is Julian. Shaffer's stage
directions provide a wealth of physical details and mannerisms for the comical detective. Julian is described as
possessing '*a gentle eccentricity, a nervousness combined
with an air of almost meek self-disapprobation, and a
certain bright detachment*'. Shaffer further describes him
as wearing a stereotyped – indeed, parodic – white trench
coat containing many pockets. Out of those pockets the
sleuth continually retrieves packets of raisins and nuts to
nibble. The battered attaché case he carries never serves
as a repository for crucial legal papers but is his catch-all
for personal items. In some ways the figure of Julian
Cristoforou resembles the eccentrics (derived from the
medieval theory of 'humours') in so many comedies by
Shakespeare, Jonson, Wilde and Shaw. And, like such
quirky characters, Julian paradoxically discovers the
answers sought diligently by more sober-minded figures.
At the heart of his characterisation is a goal of remedying
problems, not just imposing justice.

A comic version of the May–December marriage lends structure to *The Public Eye*. Charles Sidley is a forty-year-old accountant recently married to Belinda, a vivacious girl of twenty-two. When the initial romance fades from their life, Charles believes the worst: that Belinda has become involved with another man. The suspicious husband hires Julian, the 'public eye' of the title, to follow Belinda and find out the truth. In the course of his investigations the sleuth discovers the essential facts behind his client's faltering marriage. Comic irony dominates when Julian, seemingly a clumsy oaf, salvages the marriage by providing candid advice to the stubborn and misguided husband. By cajoling husband and wife in turn, he transcends the role of detective to re-energize the foundering marriage. Both partners dedicate themselves to reviving their life together, and, unlike some May–December tales, Shaffer's comedy concludes on an upbeat note.

One key to the comedy is Shaffer's capacity for creating appealing characters. Julian is a likable figure whose easy-going manner causes others to underestimate him. An element of self-deprecation encourages people to drop their guards with him. Charles Sidley's pomposity strikes a sharp contrast to Julian's gentle mannerisms. Charles tolerates little contradiction from others. He snaps at Julian, 'I'm not noted for my patient disposition' (p. 116). And, when the detective comments negatively on Belinda's habits of dress, Charles takes immediate umbrage: 'Watch what you say, please. Everything my wife knows about hats, or clothes of any kind, she learned from me. . . When you criticize her taste in hats, you are criticizing me' (p. 120). Believing himself a Pygmalion, Charles actually is an egotistical prig. As he remembers the event, his courtship of Belinda was 'curious': 'Without my demanding it, of course, she surrendered her whole life to me, for remaking' (p. 123). In his sexist arrogance Charles believes that his young wife can benefit from his instruction.

Laughs arise when the two men, who represent very different values, tangle over the proper way to nurture a marriage. Belinda shows herself no willing Galatea when she appears on the scene. The middle section of the play gains humour from the repartée between the disillusioned couple. Belinda is worthy of a Shavian feminist, and she does not hesitate to express disappointment in her spouse. For one thing, she resents being left alone while Charles socialises with male cronies: 'And where were you? In a stuffy old club, surrounded by coughing old men with weak bladders and filthy tempers, scared of women and all mauve with brandy' (p. 129. She is fun-loving and is not ready to adopt her husband's routine lifestyle. She insists on retaining her individuality in married life at all costs. Charles, meanwhile, seeks to subdue her youthful buoyancy, and to get her to behave in what he considers the appropriate manner for the wife of a respected businessman. The situation is ripe to prick his pomposity.

Until Julian suggests a compromise, the marriage appears doomed. Far from being Charles's rival, Julian is the play's merry reconciling agent. His accurate diagnosis of the couple's problem centres on Charles's ill-conceived attitude toward marriage. Julian must also convince Belinda to put aside her disillusionment and try again with Charles. Interestingly, Julian's rationale touches on a recurrent motif in Shaffer's plays – namely, the need to reconcile the universal principles of instinct and order:

JULIAN.   You're Spirit, Belinda, and he's Letter. You've
got passion where all he's got is pronouncement.
BELINDA.   You're not mad. You're not mad at all. You
don't miss anything.
JULIAN.   Of course. I have a Public Eye.
BELINDA.   What else does it see?
JULIAN.   That Charles Sidley is half dead, and only his
wife can save him.   (p. 142)

In a lively conclusion, Julian presses the stodgy accountant to leave his business long enough for a second
courtship of Belinda. While the couple repair their marriage, he, Julian, will manage Charles's affairs. He steps in
for Charles with typical good humour when a client
telephones the office. Without pause, the erstwhile
detective slips into his new role as businessman: 'Well,
permit me to introduce myself. My name is Cristoforou.
Julian Cristoforou. Diplomas in Accountancy from the
Universities of Cairo, Beirut, Istanbul, and Damascus.
Author of the well-known handbook *Teach Yourself Tax
Evasion*. What seems to be your particular problem?'
(p. 147).

The Public Eye holds up well over time, and is occasionally revived. Its good-natured humour, matched with
a playful but plausible dialectic on marriage, lends
substance to the well-worn comic pattern of marital
disharmony. Still, ultimately it is the vitality of the eccentric trio of characters which constitutes the play's greatest
appeal, not a specific moral.

Notwithstanding the comic effectiveness of *The Public
Eye*, Shaffer's most indelible mark on comedy – until
Lettice & Lovage – was made by *Black Comedy*. Early in
1965, Kenneth Tynan, then dramaturg of the British

National Theatre, asked Shaffer to provide a one-acter for the company. Strindberg's *Miss Julie* was scheduled for the coming season at Chichester, and another one-act work was needed to complete the bill. Shaffer had no specific play or plot in mind; but he did remember the startling effect from a particular production of the Peking Opera. The chief device was simple but striking: darkness on stage was represented by brilliant white light, while light was indicated by total darkness instead. That technique – the reversal of light and blackout – underlay the rudimentary scenario which Shaffer took to Laurence Olivier, then directing the National. Olivier approved the concept at once, and Shaffer found himself writing his comedy.[6]

Despite scant rehearsal time, *Black Comedy* opened at the Chichester Festival on 27 July 1965 as initially intended. John Dexter directed, eliciting strong performances from Derek Jacobi (as Brindsley Miller), Albert Finney (as Harold Gorringe), Maggie Smith (as Clea) and Michael Byrne (as Georg Bamberger). Later that year the entire production transferred to the Old Vic Theatre (then the London home of the National), where it ran for many additional months. When *Black Comedy* eventually crossed the Atlantic for a Broadway production at the Ethel Barrymore Theatre (opening on 12 February 1967), it was paired with *White Liars*, a companion one-act comedy that Shaffer had written in the interim. The New York staging of the *Black Comedy* also benefited from a strong cast: Michael Crawford (Brindsley), Lynn Redgrave (Carol Melkett), Peter Bull (Colonel Melkett), Donald Madden (Harold) and Geraldine Page (Clea).

With few exceptions *Black Comedy* was widely admired. Most complaints, in fact, were about its length, judged excessive for a one-act play. Reviewers extolled the play as farce, pointing out that subtle comic touches were few and that the piece relied instead on continuous broad, physical humour. Wit, imagination and unrelenting laughter were other common descriptions in reviews of the opening. The critics who came out most strongly in favour of the play were Milton Shulman of London's *Evening Standard* (28 July 1965 and 9 March 1966), Clive Barnes in the *New York Times* (19 October 1967), John Chapman in the New York *Daily News* (13 and 19 February 1967), Harold Clurman in the *Nation* (27 February 1967), Richard Watts, Jr, in the *New York Post* (25 February 1967), Rosemary Say in the London *Sunday Telegraph* (25 February 1967), and J. R. T. in *The Times* (22 February 1967). With *Black Comedy* Shaffer once and for all proved himself expert in both serious drama and comedy.

Shaffer relies on many proven techniques in *Black Comedy*. The piece is replete with eight funny characters, misunderstandings which create hilarious confusions, and razor-sharp pacing which sets up crucial near-misses and countless pratfalls. The initial situation is simple enough. Georg Bamberger, a wealthy art-collector, expresses interest in purchasing original works by the young artist Brindsley Miller. It is a transaction which, if consummated, would make Brindsley's reputation. Consequently his aim is to win over Bamberger at all costs. As the comedy opens, Brindsley and his fiancée, Carol Melkett, are rearranging the living room of his apartment, where the play's action takes place and where Bamberger is expected to arrive at any moment. Complicating the situation is Carol's insistence that Brindsley 'borrow' his neighbour's tasteful (and expensive) furnishings to impress her stiff-backed father, Colonel Melkett, whom she has inadvisedly invited to the flat the same evening.

Harold Gorringe, the arty neighbour (who happens to have a crush on Brindsley), is assumed to be out of town for the weekend. Brindsley intends to move all the borrowed furniture back to Harold's flat as soon as the 'right' impression has been made on Colonel Melkett and the crucial negotiations are completed with Bamberger. Shaffer designs a perfect, suspenseful situation: can their innocent intrigue succeed in winning the Colonel's approval as well as Bamberger's patronage? Brindsley summarises the matter with a prayer: 'Oh, God, let this evening go all right! Let Mr Bamberger like my sculpture and buy some! Let Carol's monster father like me! And let my neighbor Harold Gorringe never find out that we borrowed his precious furniture behind his back! Amen' (pp. 189–90). It will prove a futile prayer in such a farce, of course.

But the dramatist is not working only with traditional comic materials in *Black Comedy*. Readers especially must keep in mind the Chinese theatre device of light–dark reversal. Brindsley supposedly has to shift Harold's furniture between apartments in the complete darkness caused by a blown fuse. Seen in the theatre, characters groping blindly around a brilliantly illuminated room afford opportunities for slapstick routines. Boisterous comedy results from Brindsley's mimed actions in particular. He realises the importance of keeping his secrets, first regarding Harold's furnishings and later regarding Clea's presence in the blacked-out room. Throughout the play he is seen frantically juggling furniture and people in the darkened flat. Shaffer gives explicit stage directions to indicate a variety of comic manoeuvres. To maintain his ambitious charades, Brindsley has to slink about the apartment shifting furniture (and whatever else) without anyone else knowing:

The wire of the lamp has followed BRINDSLEY *round the bottom of the rocking chair. It catches.* BRINDSLEY *tugs it gently. The chair moves. Surprised, the* COLONEL *jerks forward.* BRINDSLEY *tugs it again, much harder. The rocking chair is pulled forward, spilling the* COLONEL *out of it, again onto the floor, and then falling itself on top of him . . .* (p. 208)

The light–dark device never wears thin, because Shaffer shrewdly fills the story with eight 'humour' types to generate evolving internal conflicts and dynamics. Cause of the problem is a blown fuse which breaks the electric current to the flat. Seeking refuge from the dark in the apartment building is another of Brindsley's neighbours, Miss Furnival. She is a romantic spinster only too willing to misinterpret a man's accidentally touching her when the lights are off. There are more convolutions when Brindsley's former lover Clea unexpectedly enters the darkened apartment. She has to let Brindsley know that she is there, and he must placate her (she had not known before of his plan to marry Carol) while keeping her presence unknown to Carol. Add to the mélange the prissy homosexual Harold, who arrives without warning. Ironically, Harold is even more miffed than Clea upon hearing of Brindsley's marriage plans. Once Harold returns, Brindsley realises that he must return the furniture and art pieces immediately, before the electricity is restored. More comic confusion awaits Brindsley with the arrival of the electrician Schuppanzigh. His heavy German accent leads those imprisoned in the dark to mistake him for the awaited art patron Bamberger. (Bamberger conveniently is described as nearly deaf, allowing for still more misunderstandings when he finally does enter.)

Using dazzling farce, Shaffer approximates Jonsonian comic turmoil, in which humorously exaggerated figures interact physically within a closed space. Held captive in the same room by the darkness, the characters are put through their paces by Brindsley, who alone fully realises what is going on. Miss Furnival, ordinarily a teetotaller, is mistakenly handed an alcoholic drink, and before long she begins asking for more. Clea's presence is unknown to anyone except Brindsley, and she plays pranks on those assembled in darkness. Eventually she makes herself known to the others after paying back Brindsley for his refusal to marry her. In a brilliant device which underscores how little people truly know one another, Clea initiates a game in the dark whereby each person is to guess who sits next to him or her by the feel of the hand. Total chaos takes place when only Harold can correctly identify the hand of the person adjacent to him in the blackness:

> CLEA.   You try it, Harold. Take the hand on your right.
> HAROLD.   I'm not playing. It's a bloody silly game.
> CLEA.   Go on . . . [*She seizes his hand and puts it into* BRINDSLEY's] Well?
> HAROLD.   It's Brin.
> BRINDSLEY.   Yes.
> CLEA.   Well done! [*She sits on the low stool.*]
> CAROL.   [*outraged*]: How does he know that? How does *he* know your hand and I don't?   (p. 231)

The noose is drawn tighter around Brindsley's neck when Bamberger finally arrives – just in time to fall through the unseen trap door leading to the fuse box. By then, everyone present is furious with the young artist. When the lights eventually go on (that is, there is a blackout on stage), Brindsley has a swarm of irate guests with whom to contend.

Black Comedy marvellously combines essential comic ingredients to generate continuous laughter. Shaffer engineers a foolproof comic situation in which Brindsley, the ostensible hero of the piece, uses pretence to gain his goal. His less than total honesty with almost everyone – especially Clea, Carol, Bamberger, Harold and the Colonel – guarantees him difficulties; and, like someone trying to plug a series of leaks, he is shown racing from one emergency spot to the next. The dark–light switch is Shaffer's ultimate secret weapon. Brindsley is depicted in ridiculous poses and contortions while attempting the impossible logistics of exchanging furniture between adjacent apartments while also maintaining lively conversation with a room full of visitors – all to be accomplished in total darkness. The slapstick body movements, however, are nearly matched by the exceptionally ironic and witty dialogue sustained throughout the wildly kinetic action of the play. Ultimately, of course, boy will get girl. Brindsley and Clea will patch up their affair after the episode in the dark proves Carol an inappropriate wife for Brindsley.

A romp from first to last, *Black Comedy* can claim to be one of the funniest farces of the twentieth century. It continues to be staged all over the world, and Shaffer fully expects a major new production in London or New York some time in the future. He has thought of expanding the text into two acts – ironically, a plan that he discarded earlier in the play's history. What will be missing in future stagings, however, is the genius of the original director, the late John Dexter, for translating a printed script into brilliant theatre. Few theatre critics deny the crucial part played by Dexter's firm directorial guidance in the success of *Royal Hunt*, *Black Comedy* and later *Equus*. Shaffer acknowledges that, without Dexter to concoct ingenious comic stage business, a truly winning new production of *Black Comedy* will be more difficult. But, in whatever format, *Black Comedy* is likely to retain its popularity, because its outrageous situations and comical characters remain archetypal, hence universal.

When it was decided to take *Black Comedy* to Broadway, Shaffer chose to write another one-act comedy as companion piece rather than augment it into a full-length play. That new one-acter, called *White Lies*, opened together with *Black Comedy* at the Ethel Barrymore Theatre, New York, on 12 February 1967. John Dexter directed the three-person play, which featured Geraldine Page (Sophie, the fortune-teller), Donald Madden (Frank) and Michael Crawford (Tom). Despite an able cast and strong direction, *White Lies* proved disappointing. Whereas *Black Comedy* inspired accolades, its counterpart elicited middling support at best from theatregoers and critics. Reviews ran distinctly on the negative side. Shaffer himself acknowledges the weaknesses of that original production. In his Preface to the *Collected Plays* he writes of *White Lies*, 'But I am afraid that I did not manage to get it quite right. The dramatic pulse was too low, and the work came out a little mechanically' (p. xiii).

Shaffer's unhappiness with the script led him to rewrite the play – not once but twice. Each time the author felt that he had come closer to his true intentions for the play, and to this day he expresses faith in its central concept. The second version, entitled *The White Liars*, opened in London in 1968 at the Lyric Theatre. This time Peter Wood directed, with Ian McKellen in the role of Tom. Shaffer was most satisfied with the third version, called *White Liars*. It is this preferred text which he included in his *Collected Plays*. But, even reworked several times, *White Lies / The White Liars / White Liars* comes across as contrived and sterile. The characters Tom and Frank undergo major transformations from the first version to the third. Still, even taking into consideration the shifting illusions of this detective comedy, there remain unclear factors associated with the two men. Tom and Frank evolve as integers in an equation, as cyphers who rarely touch us as convincing figures. Sophie also is altered from one version to the next, yet in her case Shaffer maintains audience interest. The background given Sophie suggests interesting resonances (e.g. how much of her public image is factual, how much fictional?). We can relate to her even if not approve of her actions. The neatness of story line in the other comedies is absent from *White Liars*, suggesting that Shaffer was not absolutely certain what direction he wanted his play to take. Yet the initial concept of the piece is arresting, and the figure of Sophie has appeal, so the play does offer some dramatic rewards.

Peter Shaffer's longstanding interest in the mystery genre resurfaces in *White Liars*. The story concerns a bogus fortune-teller, Baroness Sophie Lemberg, whose moth-eaten parlour sits on the pier of a desolate seaside resort on England's south coast. The plot revolves around her dealings with two young men who stop in her shop supposedly to have their fortunes told. However, it becomes evident that each wants more than the fictions of a fortune-teller. In talking with the 'Baroness', the men offer contradictory assertions. The play is transformed into a detective story when she seeks to learn who is telling the truth and what each youth is after. Like most mystery stories, *White Liars* provides alternative versions of the truth which the 'detective' must sort out. And in typical Shaffer style the conclusion involves a major surprise.

After creating a gloomy mood with a foggy setting, Shaffer proceeds to build his characters, beginning with Sophie, who calls herself the Baroness Lemberg. Down and out, the fake clairvoyant sits swilling gin and complaining to herself of life's injustices. Unexpectedly, people approach, and she preens herself for the pending clients, two young men. Each has a question for her. Frank, the more clean-cut of the two, demands to talk first with the Baroness; Tom, the other youth – unkempt and in 'trendy' clothes – agrees to return later. After testing Sophie's suitability, Frank admits why he really has come. He wants her, in her capacity of clairvoyant, to play an innocent trick on Tom: 'You see, I've – I've got a suggestion. A sort of a – little game. A, well, frankly a . . . look, Baroness, I don't really want my fortune told at all. I've come about something entirely different' (p. 157). Sophie at first refuses but consents to the charades when Frank offers sufficient financial inducement. According to Frank, Tom has fallen for Frank's girlfriend, and Frank wants Sophie to frighten off his rival with a threatening 'fortune' if Tom persists. Frank provides Sophie sufficient background about Tom to make her phony prophecy credible.

When Tom enters, Sophie uses Frank's 'inside information' to impress him and win his confidence. She builds a menacing argument using Frank's information and seemingly wins Tom over. Just when Sophie thinks she has fulfilled Frank's objectives, Shaffer pulls his first surprise. Sophie has repeated Frank's story accurately, but Frank was totally wrong on the facts. Tom, it seems, has been deliberately misleading his chum. Tom stuns the Baroness when he states 'From the moment Frank came in here he handed you a pack of lies. One after another' (p. 173). Tom unsuccessfully tries to discredit Frank, but Sophie by then is so involved in Frank's fable that she cannot believe Tom nor the truth.

When Tom abruptly departs, Shaffer follows with his second – and most stunning – revelation. Sue, the unseen girl in the story, is not Frank's girlfriend at all. Frank and Tom have been homosexually involved, and Tom has intimated that he is going to leave Frank for the girl. Frank therefore wants the match between Tom and Sue broken off for reasons quite different from those he claimed at first. The Baroness finally grasps the situation when Frank tells her, 'I wanted him to leave her alone! . . . And to stay with me. In – my – bed' (p. 177). Sophie is left to contemplate the slipperiness of facts and the illusions dominating her own life. She shouts to Frank 'Take comfort, mister – here's a bit of comfort. It's not only the young who lie, whatever I said, it's not true – the old are worse. They are the biggest liars of them all! He [Sophie's husband] was not a Baron; I am not a Baroness; my mother was not a Romany noblewoman, she was just a gypsy – and not even interesting' (p. 178).

Shaffer believes that *White Liars* will gain a new lease of life, perhaps even in another format. Notwithstanding occasional infelicities in the writing, the play inventively treats materials not found in his other comedies. The illusion-and-reality dynamic may not be wholly novel, but until this piece Shaffer had reserved its use for his more serious dramas. In *White Liars* Shaffer succeeds in wringing laughter from the illusions that the three characters try to foist on each other. The suspense element works effectively in *White Liars* to create baffling characters and surprise disclosures. Most memorable is Sophie, who like a comic Mother Courage muddles her way through a life filled with uncertainties. Interestingly, David Mamet in analogous fashion would later employ a deceptive clairvoyant as the central feature of his short play *The Shawl*, as Noel Coward had done in *Blithe Spirit*. Intriguing figures that they are, spiritualists and witches have appeared, as an energising force, in dramas of all periods. Shaffer therefore wants to make *White Liars* into a movie or perhaps a television drama. He believes that, beside the interest elicited by having a medium at the centre, the unique seaside atmosphere lends itself superbly to the camera, where theatrical devices are limitless. Meanwhile, the comedy offers a star turn for actresses playing the eccentric Baroness Lemberg, clairvoyant, whose ironic motto is 'Lemberg Never Lies'.

Some of the dramatic problems that limit the effectiveness of *White Liars* also diminish *The Battle of Shrivings*, Shaffer's only total failure on stage. Again, a bloodless story centres on characters devoid of sympathy. Cast with top-flight performers (John Gielgud, Wendy Hiller, Dorothy Lyman and Patrick Magee) and directed by Peter Hall, *The Battle of Shrivings* opened to high expectations at London's Lyric Theatre (February 1970). Shaffer relates the painful results in 'A Note on the Play, 1974'. The drama elicited universal criticism and closed within a few weeks. Later Shaffer rewrote the work completely. The printed version, called *Shrivings*, appeared four years after the original staging, but to date it has received no major commercial production.

Several problems surface in *Shrivings*, the text Shaffer selected for his *Collected Plays*. The story-telling structure, a modified naturalism, is uninventive and brittle. The opening scenes are blatantly expository, and the predictable central conflict generates only modest suspense. Tension is further lessened by the absence of characters who interest us. Each character exhibits major personality flaws derived from unconvincing motivation; nor do genuinely likable characters appear in the drama. A dozen years after the initial staging, Shaffer contemplated the facts coolly: 'It seemed to me, on reflection, that there was a danger in my work of theme dictating event, and that a strong impulse to compose rhetorical dialectic was beginning to freeze my characters into theoretical attitudes' (Preface, p. xiv). The playwright's analysis is accurate. His characters manifest little dramatic life of their own, remaining mere voices for the author's polemics.

Shaffer has declared his topic to be the idea of human improvability. The search for perfectibility underlying *Royal Hunt* is here turned down a notch because (as Shaffer's Note explains) the idealism of the radical peace movement in the 1960s and 1970s aroused outpourings both of altruism and of hatred. Shaffer fashions two antipodal characters to embody the head-on confrontation between faith and cynical disbelief. One protagonist is Sir Gideon Petrie, guru head of a world peace organisation; his philosophical premise is that human beings are improvable and that their faulty conduct can be ameliorated. Countering Petrie is a renowned poet named Mark Askelon, who as a youth had been Gideon's protégé. Nurtured by their spiritual relationship, the younger man's poetic artistry flourished and won him an international reputation. Askelon, cynical and burnt-out when the play opens, returns years later to visit his old mentor. The heart of the plot concerns Mark's spiritual turnabout which leads him to challenge Gideon's life values.

Gideon's headquarters, called Shrivings, are ancient buildings in England once used as a religious retreat.

From there Gideon conducts a world-wide campaign on behalf of universal peace. The epitome of the altruistic 'do-gooder', he attracts followers from all countries. Mark meanwhile has become jaded and debauched by success. His is a soul consumed by scepticism. The corrosiveness of Mark's negativism appears early in the drama, when he converses with Gideon's personal secretary Lois:

MARK.   What's a saint?

LOIS.   A man who doesn't know what it is to reject people.

MARK.   And that's Gideon?

LOIS.   He has no hostility left in him for anyone in the world.

MARK.   Do you really believe that?

LOIS.   Absolutely. He's proved it can be done.

(p. 327)

This early crossing of swords sets up the major collision of values to follow. To Mark, his old friend's unwavering belief in 'doing good' is naïve and misleading to followers. The mocking poet believes that Gideon's self-sacrificing crusade creates a phony idealism concerning a flawed universe. But a more important reason why Mark is eager to prove Gideon false is that his own son, David (whom he abandoned), has joined the Shrivings community. David has consciously chosen Gideon as his spiritual father. By that act, he has tacitly rejected Mark, his blood father. David also symbolises 'the future' and so becomes the centre of contention in the forming battle. Mark's desire to expose Gideon's failings thus goes beyond simple personal disagreements. Like an archetypal Satan, Mark intends to fight for the hearts and souls of Gideon's proselytes.

Theoretically several well-defined dualities should assure vitality for the plot of *Shrivings*. And on paper the story line possesses points of interest. For instance, both Lois and David become hostage in the contest between Gideon and his former disciple. When the play begins, the two young believers are wholly committed to Gideon's philosophy, and they defend their idol from Mark's gibes. When ordinary ridicule fails to weaken Gideon's moral grasp, Mark precipitates the play's eventual showdown by challenging the guru to a direct contest of good versus evil. Mark announces his proposal at the close of the first act:

GIDEON.   What do you know?

MARK.   That the Gospel According to Saint Gideon is a lie. That we as men cannot alter for the better in any particular that matters. That we are totally and forever unimprovable. . . . We are made of hostility as the spring is made of pollen. And each birth renews it, as the spring renews the year.

GIDEON.   No.

MARK.   Prove it. . . . I propose a battle. It is now Friday night. I say by Monday morning . . . you will have thrown me out of Shrivings. How about that?
(pp. 347–8)

Gideon confidently accepts the challenge, saying, 'Stay in this house as long as you wish. Shrivings will never reject you' (p. 348). Shaffer's typical challenge between man and alleged supernatural power momentarily furnishes the plot with suspense.

Shrivings then changes in tempo and texture. Mark's efforts to make his presence unbearable fail when

Gideon's firm pacifism keeps his emotions in check. Verbal insults, mockery and temptations all have no effect, and Mark must resort to unscrupulous measures. He easily – too easily – seduces Lois, later flaunting the fact before his son David, who himself harbours incipient feelings of love for her. Bewildered by her guilt, Lois loses her grip on faith in 'the good'. David's beliefs also increasingly are shaken by his father's arbitrary cruelty. Mark finally wins his battle with Gideon by maliciously announcing the older man's longstanding homosexuality. The *coup de grâce* is given when Mark insinuates that the master's attentions to David reflect sensual, not spiritual, motives. The unmitigated evil in Mark's statements ultimately turn Gideon and Lois against each other (Gideon ends up slapping her hard, twice). Mark achieves his evil goal when David rejects Gideon as a fake. In great disillusionment, the youth abandons his guru to join his father in an illusionless world.

The conclusion of *Shrivings* is meant to display the victory of evil over any possibility for good. Human beings are seemingly capable of amoral actions, and an unacceptably high price is paid for succumbing to one's darker self. But the ending, like the play in its entirety, does not ring true. The closing scene is puzzling. Mark the victor pleads for a final benediction (forgiveness? understanding?) from Gideon, the very victim whom he has discredited and destroyed. The scene is reminiscent of Pizarro's last disillusioned outburst to the corpse of Atahuallpa in *Royal Hunt*. But here Mark's motives are unclear and his language excessive. He rails,

> Here! This tool for making. A killer's hand. It's all you've got . . . Take it.

[GIDEON *ignores it, staring straight ahead*]
What will it do without you? Squeeze some more
napalm out of my cock? Drive more Red tanks over
dreaming heads? Wear the Pope's ring, and dip a
gold pen in the sick of starving children it's helped to
create? . . . Have you no word for me? No word at
all?

GIDEON.   Dust. (pp. 393–4)

In terms of plot, Shaffer employs materials which
conceivably can produce important drama. However,
fundamental problems militate against the success of
Shrivings, and chief of these are contrived motivations for
what are essentially puppet figures. Characters become
integers in a mathematical formula representing good and
evil, not people snared in real-life dilemmas. Mark Askelon stands out as a problematic character because, though
his antipathy for Gideon is clear enough, the play offers
no explanation of how he changed so radically from
youthful idealism to adult scepticism. A comparable difficulty arises in *White Liars* for similar reasons: characters
are given insufficient motives and they thereby cannot
enlist deep audience interest. Patches of overwritten
dialogue undermine dramatic tension here, too, as in
White Liars previously and as in *Yonadab* later. Shaffer's
plays come close to being pretentious when his language
becomes overheated – a fact of which he is aware. Moreover, the script of *Shrivings* runs longer than even that
of *Royal Hunt*, a more action-filled parable on a related
subject. *Shrivings* alerted Shaffer to the potential length
problem of his plays. When making major revisions later
in his career, he has always tightened up his scripts. Had
another playwright written *Shrivings*, critical disappointment might have been muted; but given Shaffer's strong

preceding dramas, expectations were greater than either *The Battle of Shrivings* or *Shrivings* could meet. Even some rough patches during this twelve-year period would not deter him, however. He learned much from both his newly developed comic ability and from occasional mistakes. Each play from this building period would have its role in shaping the fine works of his mature career.

4
Widening the Creative Lens: 'The Royal Hunt of the Sun'

The Royal Hunt of the Sun (1964) marks a watershed in Peter Shaffer's early career. Thematically and technically, the drama departs radically from Shaffer's well-behaved plays of social realism. In *Royal Hunt*, the playwright expanded philosophical themes on an epic scale, employing 'larger-than-life' dialogue to weld together an episodic story expressed through stylised representational techniques. The theatrically adventurous Peter Shaffer we recognise today appears for the first time in *The Royal Hunt of the Sun*.

Ironically, *Royal Hunt* existed in draft form even before *Five Finger Exercise* first opened. In interviews and in the Preface to the *Collected Plays* Shaffer gives a full explanation of his preference for stylised theatre over naturalism. In a BBC radio interview of 11 September 1979 he admits a lifelong love of Shakespearean dramas, of 'big, sweeping theatre' in the epic tradition. From the beginning of his career Shaffer wanted to write plays that were 'part of the grandiloquent and showy world of imaginative reality' (Preface, p. x).[1] But, he adds, 'The mid-1950s did not constitute a time when one could admit . . . a purpose to write about gods and grand aspirations, orations and ecstatics' (p. x). Because naturalistic drama then dominated British stages, it took several years for *Royal Hunt* to be produced. Moreover, its staging requirements, which are demanding and costly, make it a calculated risk for producers in any period. Nearly three dozen actors are called for by the script; and the set design requires utmost ingenuity to capture the exotic qualities demanded by Shaffer's stage directions.

Frightened off by the staging expenses, the Royal Shakespeare Company (whom Shaffer had in mind when writing the script) passed up an option on *Royal Hunt*. Eventually the fledgling National Theatre accepted the play, when director John Dexter chose it from a pile of submitted scripts. Audiences responded enthusiastically when the play opened at the Chichester Festival, on 7 July 1964. Colin Blakely and Robert Stephens won special praise for their portrayals of Pizarro and Atahuallpa; playing lesser roles were Derek Jacobi, Michael Byrne and Edward Petherbridge, all of whom have since become mainstays of the British stage. In that autumn the entire production moved to the Old Vic Theatre in London. An equally well-cast and acclaimed production opened in New York at the ANTA Theatre on 26 October 1965. Christopher Plummer and David Carradine played Pizarro and Atahuallpa, with George Rose as the adult Martin Ruiz. Seven producers pooled their resources to mount this production – the expense involved being one reason the work is not staged more frequently, as Shaffer has recognised.

Critical as well as popular reaction to *Royal Hunt* was unusually warm. Bernard Levin claimed that 'no greater play has been written and produced . . . in my lifetime' (London *Daily Mail*). Martin Esslin deemed it 'a first rate text: witty, wise and well written' (*Plays and Players*). A minority viewpoint was expressed by Martin Gottfried, who labelled *Royal Hunt* a 'very ceremonial, very ritualistic, very spectacular bore' (*Women's Wear Daily*). Although British reviewers, with few exceptions, were satisfied with the play, Shaffer was not. As customary with him, he did not feel the script wholly finished and continued to rework it, chiefly through trimming. Most observers considered the New York version to be improved, and American critics lauded it as an exciting and important work.[2]

Two essential characteristics of Shaffer's writing emerge fully developed for the first time in *Royal Hunt*. Thematically, Pizarro manifests the archetypical Shafferian protagonist seeking a knowable deity to lend rational order to the chaotic universe. Askelon, Dysart, Salieri and Yonadab play comparable roles in subsequent dramas. Uniting the historian's eye with that of the dramatist, Shaffer discerns aspects of Inca civilisation relevant to the play's intellectual and spiritual questions. The result is historical revisionism driven by dramaturgical needs. Shaffer refocuses – even distorts – seminal historical accounts to present audiences with a new, often iconoclastic perspective. By combining the character's individual quest with events from cultural history, he transforms historical episodes into formative experiences for a questing hero. Unlikely historical figures (Pizarro, Salieri, Yonadab) thus turn up in Shaffer's dramas as metaphysical pilgrims. As a backdrop to the philosophical probings, civilisations and cultures are shown colliding, casting traditional reli-

gious and political premises into doubt. Shaffer's unorthodox handling of historical data suggests a need to redefine
the external human predicament. But his approach dis-
mays those unable to relate imaginatively to his dramatic
parables. More recently, *Amadeus* has been publicly
criticised for taking liberties with history. In part for his
dramaturgical manipulation of history, Shaffer continues
to be a controversial figure in the world of theatre.

Royal Hunt also signals a shift in the stage techniques
required by Shaffer's scripts. From this point on, his plays
frequently forgo literal representation in favour of a more
stylised, epic approach. Pageantry, ritual, music, masks,
choreographed dance and mimes – features central to the
'total theatre' he has long admired – create powerful stage
emblems to convey fable on a non-literal plane. Gone is
the social realism of *Five Finger Exercise* (with its cast of
five) and of the one-acters. Except in the disappointing
Batte of Shrivings and the dazzling farces *Black Comedy*
and *Lettice & Lovage*, Shaffer after *Royal Hunt* abandons
conventional naturalism. Long before *Royal Hunt*, in fact,
he expressed dissatisfaction with the restrictions imposed
by naturalism in the theatre. When asked by *The Sunday
Times* in 1958 about his aesthetic biases, Shaffer replied, 'I
want to revive the magic and the rhetoric, all the things
that make the audience go "Ooh!" We've surrendered too
much to the cinema and we've got to get some of it back.'[3]
Given the continued popularity of *Royal Hunt*, Shaffer's
belief in unrestricted theatricality appears well war-
ranted.[4]

To measure the significance of the play's subject, the
earthshaking consequences of its central conflict must be
considered. Like historians before him, Shaffer was stag-
gered by the amazing events that had unfolded in South
America early in the sixteenth century, when representat-

ives of the European Holy Roman Empire took on the Inca Empire in a fight to the death. Unbelievably, through guile and betrayal just 167 Spaniard warriors succeeded in vanquishing and subjugating the gigantic Inca realm. The King of Spain, Charles V, also was Emperor of the Holy Roman Empire; to gain popular support for his far-flung military adventures, he used his religious title to gloss over blatantly imperialistic objectives. Shaffer's play, set in the period 1529–33, follows Charles's agents Francisco Pizarro and his men during their second tour of duty in the New World. Pizarro's earlier sojourn in South America had confirmed the existence of vast, untapped wealth. Their return trip would bring the Spaniards general riches and fame, while extending Spain's empire into the newly discovered hemisphere.

It is a native civilisation of immense size and power which awaits the invading Spaniards. Within the time-frame of the play, 6 million natives representing one hundred tribes are ruled by Atahuallpa. Calling himself immortal son of the sun god, Atahuallpa, like his European counterparts, is adept at using religion to further his political ambitions. He has blood on his hands, having assassinated his brother to gain the throne, yet he and his peoples are completely unprepared for the savagery of the foreign invaders. Pretending to come in peace, the conquistadors seize Atahuallpa and butcher hundreds of his unarmed men. The bewildered Indians collect a huge ransom in gold to secure the release of their king–god, but when it is paid the Spaniards callously kill Atahuallpa and put an end to an empire which has lasted 2000 years.[5]

Shaffer says that most of his factual material derives from W. H. Prescott's nineteenth-century classic *The History of the Conquest of Peru*.[6] While not a political activist in the manner of Arden, Hare or Bond, Shaffer none the less sensed in Prescott's accounts the cynical brutality inherent in the building of an empire. Shaffer is even-handed in portraying the momentous confrontation between Europe and the New World. Both factions are shown guilty of seizing and retaining power at the expense of ordinary citizens. Political *Leitmotives*, then, underlie the play, leavening the overall psychodrama.

The story told in *Royal Hunt* begins with Pizarro recruiting men in Spain, and concludes several years later in Cajamarca with the garrotting of Atahuallpa. Shaffer retains the basic historical outline without hesitating to inset entirely fictional episodes for dramatic purposes. Two acts, each comprised of twelve scenes, provide the framework. Act I focuses on civilised man's limitless lust for wealth – the symbolic hunt for gold; Act II concentrates on man's instinctive quest for eternal life – that is, the search for an immortal deity. The action is continuous, scenes unfolding without pause. A prologue narrated by Pizarro's erstwhile aide Martin Ruiz announces the theme. In gloomy soliloquy, Martin looks back at earlier events to explain, 'This story is about ruin. Ruin and gold . . . I'm going to tell you how one hundred and sixty-seven men conquered an empire of twenty-four million' (p. 247). Europe's triumph over the Indians brought not ecstasy, Martin insists, but despair.

Much of Act I (entitled 'The Hunt') uses imaginative pantomime and stylised combat to tell what is essentially an adventure story. Pizarro rouses his rag-tag mercenaries, who, once in the new World, undertake a perilous mimed trek across the Andes to meet with Atahuallpa at Cajamarca. Thanks to Pizarro's incessant prodding, and to their limitless lust for gold, the Spaniards climb the difficult trail to rendezvous with the sun king. When Atahuallpa fails to appreciate the lunatic nerve of Pizarro and his men, the unarmed Incas are easily slaughtered by the Spaniards. Only the king and a handful of counsellors are spared. Although individualised and romanticised, the basic facts are accurate to this point. Act II ('The Kill') focuses on Atahuallpa's imprisonment for several months, during which the Spanish general and his captive undergo a powerful process of male bonding. Here Shaffer's version of events is entirely fictional; no historical evidence suggests that the rival leaders ever developed a personal relationship.

From the perspective of Shaffer's career, the figure of Francisco Pizarro inaugurates a succession of god-seeking protagonists through whom the dramatist explores teleological questions. Though the issues introduced by such characters may not be philosophically complex, they entail fundamental human concerns. The subject of death versus immortality dominates the play. Death, the eternal enigma, often drives Shaffer's protagonists to search for a beneficent deity tending the universe. But, to make Pizarro function dramatically as a prototypical hunter of God, Shaffer radically alters the facts. Early in the play, Pizarro appears alert and reflective despite a brutish exterior. De Soto, a confidant who provides reliable insights throughout the play, recognises that something other than gold spurs Pizarro on. That something is Pizarro's growing obsession with the inexorable onward march of time, with death the inescapable end. Pizarro – Shaffer's Everyman – complains bitterly of man's unfair status in the physical world: 'Time whipped up the lust in me and Time purged it. I was dandled on Time's knee and made to gurgle, then put to my sleep. I've been cheated from the moment I was born because there's death in everything' (p. 272). To which, significantly, De Soto responds, 'Except in God.' But Shaffer's Pizarro can no longer rely on the traditional Christian God, because the Church's corruption is evidenced everywhere around him. Thus for Pizarro the answer – if one exists at all – must be found elsewhere. Shaffer shapes Pizarro's encounter with Atahuallpa as the catalyst in the Spaniard's search for a god. The title of Act I, 'The Hunt', signifies both the hunt for gold in the New World and a personal inner search for a deity.

Historically, the conquistadors pursued the Inca sun king for his power and riches. In Shaffer's dramatic calculus, Atahuallpa also manifests answers to Pizarro's metaphysical riddles. At first the king is simply Pizarro's military adversary. As he comes to know his extraordinary captive better, however, Pizarro is attracted to Atahuallpa's unassailable self-assurance. In matters of society, politics and religion, he is arrogantly certain of the answers. And, although sceptical at first, Pizarro comes to see the Inca king's beliefs as offering a last hope of discerning an ultimate design in human life. Pizarro declares of his prisoner, 'He has some meaning for me, this man-god. An immortal man in whom all his people live completely. He has an answer for Time' (p. 282).

Pizarro's conversion to Atahuallpa's values does not occur instantaneously, and much of the second act is given over to charting changes in the Spaniard. Shaffer's intentions here are clear enough: namely, to convince the audience as well as Pizarro of the better, more natural lifestyle of the natives.[7] Still, the rationalisations are sometimes gratuitous. Atahuallpa, for instance, didactically insists that the Inca social system is superior to the European: everyone marries at the age of twenty-five and retires at fifty, after which he is taken care of by the state. Unlike the average destitute Spaniard, the Inca citizen has a secure place in a benevolent communist system. Each native is assigned a particular task, no job being more prestigious than any other. Such discussion of economic or political theory possesses an abstract interest, but tends to diffuse the thematic focus of the drama. Polemics at such times supersede dramatics.

But on one issue – comparative religion – Shaffer integrates clever dialectic with the core theme. Throughout the play institutional Roman Catholicism is portrayed as hopelessly corrupt: its goal in the New World is to seize wealth and power, not unlike the political state. Pizarro's spiritual malaise reflects a weary scepticism about the promises of Christianity. He grows increasingly alarmed at the absoluteness of time and its loss as he ages. Without belief in the European faith into which he was born, he is left to seek an alternative religion or metaphysical system. Atahuallpa's certitude regarding universal truths magnetically draws Pizarro to him. The King is as confident in *his* metaphysical values as Pizarro is sceptical of those of a jaded Europe. When arguing for the superiority of his cosmos, Atahuallpa saves his greatest scorn for the Europeans' organised religions. In one scene he mocks the way in which the white man's god enters his worshippers: 'They eat him. First he becomes a biscuit, and then they eat him . . . At praying they say "This is the body of our God". Then they drink his blood. [*Loftily.*] It is very bad. Here in my empire we do not eat men. My family forbade it many years past' (p. 285).

Bonding between the spiritual duellists occurs gradually throughout the second act, beginning with an exchange of tokens to celebrate their mutual bastardy and progressing to a wild dance in which they affirm their developing brotherhood. As his admiration for his hostage grows, Pizarro is won over to Atahuallpa. Late in the play he excitedly declares, 'I've gone god-hunting and caught one . . . A being who can renew his life over and over . . .' (p. 306). Shaffer abandons his historical moorings here, incorporating into his protagonists' alliance the physicality of warriors and the intellectualism of philosophers. Once convinced that the Incas pursue a more worthy godhead than Christians do, Pizarro can articulate his conversion: 'Look: I'm a peasant, I want value for money. If I go marketing for gods, who do I buy? The God of Europe with all its death and blooding, or Atahuallpa of Peru? His spirit keeps an empire sweet and still as corn in the field' (p. 303).

The fictitious brotherhood between Pizarro and Atahuallpa is introduced strictly for dramatic ends. One further dilemma demands proof of unflinching faith from each. Pizarro had sworn to release his prisoner without harm once the ransom in gold is delivered. Yet all recognise that the Inca king, once free, will order the entire Spanish contingent slain. The mercenaries are not worried, because they do not intend to release Atahuallpa alive. And, without the leadership of their god king, according to Incan tradition the Indians will be left helpless. The dilemma persists for Pizarro, however. If he releases his hostage, the Spaniards will be slain, if he reneges on his oath to free Atahuallpa, he violates his sacred word. More importantly, he then betrays and condemns to death his spiritual saviour and brother.

Shaffer twists the plot even tighter. Pizarro chooses to die with Atahuallpa rather than to betray him, but finds the sun king surprisingly unperturbed. Atahuallpa trusts in his own godhead, reassuring his friend, 'It is no matter. They cannot kill me.' For Pizarro, Atahuallpa's metaphysical stance answers the riddle of time and death: 'It's the only way to give life meaning! To blast out of Time and live forever, *us*, in our own persons! This is the law: die in

83

despair or be a god yourself!' (p. 306). Pizarro can share the godhead Atahuallpa promises by simply believing unconditionally. Pizarro accepts Atahuallpa's offer: 'Believe in me . . . For you I will do a great thing. I will swallow death and spit it out of me' (p. 307).

The close of *Royal Hunt* returns to history, and it depicts no happy ending. In a shattering final *coup de théâtre*, Atahuallpa is ritualistically garroted. Despite his assurances, no supernatural force revives Atahuallpa, and a stunned Pizarro witnesses his own metaphysical hopes be dashed. Disillusionment gives way to paroxysms of fury as Pizarro admits the futility of his search for a trustworthy god. He shouts at the king's corpse, 'Cheat! You've cheated me! Cheat . . . God's just a name on your nail; and naming begins cries and cruelties. But to live without hope of after, and make whatever God there is, oh, that's some immortal business surely!' (pp. 309–10).

The title of Act II, 'The Kill', accurately mirrors the action on two levels: the assassination of the Inca god king, and the destruction of Pizarro's hopes for godhead on this earth. When interviewed by John Russell Taylor, Peter Shaffer spoke about the crucial duality in *Royal Hunt*, which he describes as

> a play about two men: one of them is an atheist, and the other is a god . . . Pizzaro is, like most orthodox religious people, in practice an atheist: he believes, vaguely, in God, but sees him as something right outside the universe and essentially irrelevant to it and to everyday dealings in the world. Atahuallpa . . . is a god: to his people he is ruler, master, and immediately the source of all benefits, and also the embodiment of the sun, the giver of all life.[8]

'Finding oneself', along with other generational concerns treated in *Five Finger Exercise*, expands here into a probing of universal enigmas. The core theme of *Royal Hunt*, again according to Shaffer, is 'the search for god . . . the search for a definition of the idea of god'.[9] Although the playwright extends his thematic reach exponentially with *The Royal Hunt of the Sun*, not all audiences leave the theatre convinced by its religious or philosophical arguments. Parallels between Pizarro's spiritual search and the Spaniards' hunt for gold can seem forced. By speculating on matters as broad (and ambiguous) as love, religion, death, politics and life all in one play, Shaffer denies the story a secure centre point.

For many playgoers the chief source of the drama's effectiveness lies in its potential for spectacular theatricality, the aspect of it that universally thrills audiences.[10] Shaffer states his production intentions explicitly in the Author's Notes published with the playtext. To gain sweep and spectacle in plays, he explains, he turns to 'epic' and 'total' theatre, wherein 'not only words but rites, mimes, masks, and magics' are combined. Antonin Artaud (*The Theatre and its Double*) has been the most articulate proponent of 'total theatre' in the modern age, and Shaffer gains inspiration from the daring Frenchman. In 1964, in fact, Shaffer joined Peter Brook, Peter Hall, Charles Marowitz and Michel St Denis in a round table discussion of Artaud's concepts. He has most overtly followed Artaud in shaping drama as ritualistic enactment.[11] In the Preface to the *Collected Plays* he alludes to non-literal connections between performer and spectator: 'stage actors possess a sacredotal quality' because they 'are partially created by audiences whom they simultaneously partially create' (p. xi). To construct a bridge to the theatregoer, the playwright concentrates on the senses of sight and hearing. In *Royal Hunt* these are treated to an astonishing stream of (striking effects.) Brilliantly coloured Indian costumes using plumes and metallic ornaments capture the audience's eye; stylised masks with haunting eyes lend the power of ritual to suspenseful scenes such as Atahuallpa's murder. Unsettling jungle-like sounds are written into the script, and hummed music and eerie native chanting punctuate the drama at appropriate moments. Sounds are choreographically matched with visual images to produce a comprehensive assault on the senses. Marc Wilkinson's 'remarkable score (Shaffer's description) adds a continuous sound underlay to the work, imparting an orchestrated cohesiveness to the plot.

Exotic symbols and metaphors provide comparable visual coherence, as required by the author's stage directions. Most memorable is the elevated platform up-stage, an area usually reserved for action by the Incas. Given the panoramic effect required by the plot, specific geographical locations need to be designated. And because much of the opening act deals with the Spaniards' upward trek toward Cajamarca, where they meet the Inca king, it is appropriate that the invaders begin in the main stage level. From their vantage point above, the natives peer down upon the ascending intruders, who in mime climb laboriously upward to their fateful rendezvous. By placing the Indians on the upper plane during the Mime of the Great Ascent, Shaffer visually reinforces the pure isolation of the Peruvian realm high in the Andes.

Suspended above the main stage, against the back wall of the Inca space, is the play's most unforgettable emblem: a gigantic metallic disc. It is symmetrically pierced with swords to form a Christian cross for scenes on the main stage involving the conquistadors. But, when the action concerns the Incas, the disc unfolds to form giant golden petals – a blazing symbol of the Peruvian world where the sun is universal god. Meantime, the space within the disc's circumference variously represents Atahuallpa's throne room, his prison and eventually the treasure chamber. The same hanging structure is transformed into a dazzling visual metaphor in Act II, when, in a mimed section called the Second Gold Procession, the Indians gather gold artifacts to ransom Atahuallpa. As the gold pieces are systematically hung on the disc, the sunburst frame becomes increasingly gold-laden and tempting. Eventually the greedy warriors can no longer resist the accumulated booty. In a mimed scene aptly entitled the Rape of the Sun, Pizarro's soldiers savagely tear off the gold pieces, thereby plundering the golden petals and symbolically desecrating the Inca Empire.

Even more spectacular – and horrific – is the closing episode of the first act. Called the Mime of the Great Massacre, the scene presents the Spaniards' betrayal of Inca trust when the two factions meet in Cajamarca. At a stipulated signal the armed conquistadors, barely five dozen in number, attack and kill hundreds of unarmed natives. As the soldiers hew their way through the defenceless Incas in slow-motion mime, a giant blood-red cloth is extracted from the centre of the sun disc, to billow over and cover the scene of slaughter. Scenes such as this further validate Shaffer's eclecticism, which also embraces stage-combat techniques drawn from Chinese theatre. The result is a hypnotic representation of a horrifying massacre. Comparably terrible is the stylised final episode dramatising Atahuallpa's murder. For that scene grim Inca masks and frightening sounds off-stage create an unearthly backdrop for the sombre execution. Atahuallpa's people stand in the shadows around the edges of the stage, awaiting the god king's promised resurrection. Pizarro too joins the silent vigil, which continues for many minutes, until the futility of the wait is made apparent through the symbolic use of lighting. The breaking dawn gradually reveals Atahuallpa to be quite dead, still tied to the execution post, and his claims for immortality are belied for all to see. The clamour of keening Indians is paradoxically synchronised with the rise of the morning sun, which signals the extinction of the Inca Empire and the climax of Pizarro's personal tragedy.

Shaffer's text elicits an imaginative blend of visual and aural effects which continues to haunt audiences long after they have left the theatre. However, the dramatist acknowledges that much credit is due to his chief colla-borator on this work, director John Dexter. Dexter's fresh, endlessly inventive answers to the script's staging demands taught the playwright (as he admits) much about how to dramatise the printed word – how to translate it into visual terms. In his Preface to the Collected Plays Shaffer states of *Royal Hunt*, 'In the sunburst of the play's success, which certainly owed as much to the authority and passion of Dexter as to my own dream of what theatre should be like, I felt my last inhibitions dissolve' (p. xi).

With *Royal Hunt* Shaffer continued to learn his craft, and, the separate scenes making up the play suggest its episodic nature. Shaffer's eclectic approach, however, avoids excess. Alongside Dexter's influence must be set that of Bertolt Brecht, whose ideas on stage epic Shaffer has long admired: he inaugurates his own epic narrator, later perfected in Dysart (*Equus*) and Salieri (*Amadeus*). Martin Ruiz, first as a boy in the early sections and later as a mature man, serves as Pizarro's aide and as *raisonneur*. Like Shaffer's subsequent narrator figures, Martin sometimes addresses the audience directly in chorus fashion, detailing a scene with an omniscient objectivity that recalls Brecht's *Verfremdungseffekt* (alienation effect). At other times he steps back into the action of the play. Within the story Martin – played by two actors, boy and man – functions as Pizarro's alter ego and confidant. Without Martin as sounding board and idealistic counter-weight to his master, Shaffer would have had difficulty in airing Pizarro's ideas and aspirations. Also, through Martin's initial idealism, we learn of Pizarro's continued search for an ideal in life. Martin represents Pizarro's own altruism when young. Martin insists that Pizarro should keep his word to Atahuallpa by freeing him, and so reinforces the older man's dormant idealism. Shaffer does not successfully involve young Martin in all aspects of the plot, but, when the youth is present, the sweetness of his innocence provides welcome relief in an otherwise bitterly cynical story.

Perhaps Shaffer's varied theatrical means in *The Royal Hunt of the Sun* indicate a desire to thrill audiences no matter what the price. One critic observed that Shaffer 'has thrown in, with almost insolent boldness, every technique available to him, every dodge ever known to have been dramatically effective in the history of drama'.[12] When we recall the overwhelming dominance of stage naturalism at the time, we can understand possible excesses in the opposite direction. Moreover, the success of the work helped to create an audience for a more vigorously experimental drama than had been possible during the heyday of naturalism.

5
'Equus' and the Mature Shaffer

Five Finger Exercise and *The Royal Hunt of the Sun* signalled the arrival on the scene of a new, innovative voice in the theatre; *Equus* confirmed it. Shaffer's *Equus* transmutes an appalling case of animal mutilation into a universal paradigm concerning the eternal struggle between individual rights and communal demands. At the same time, the playwright continues to clarify the underlying subject of all his serious dramas: man's unending search for a dependable god who can lend order to the universe.

A chance remark to the playwright planted the seed for *Equus*. A friend at the BBC recounted certain shocking events in a country town outside London. A lad raised in a religiously repressive household had been seduced in a stable, and had reacted violently by blinding several horses kept there. From that germ sprang *Equus*. The conflict of sexual and religious beliefs offered a promising dramatic premise, but it is Shaffer's speculations on society and the individual which raise the play beyond a titillating tabloid story. Moreover, having John Dexter direct assured imaginative staging to match the provocative plot.

Equus opened on 26 July 1973 at the Old Vic Theatre, where it enjoyed an extended run in the National Theatre repertory. Alec McCowen and Peter Firth played the lead roles of the psychiatrist Martin Dysart and the troubled boy Alan Strang. A Broadway production followed, opening on 24 October 1974 at the Plymouth Theatre, with Anthony Hopkins as Dysart and Firth repeating his role as Strang. American audiences proved as enthusiastic as the British, and the New York production ran for 1209 performances – an exceptionally long run for serious drama on Broadway. During the New York run a list of distinguished actors took on the doctor's role, among them Richard Burton and Anthony Perkins. Sidney Lumet directed a controversial movie version of *Equus* (1976) based on Shaffer's own Oscar-nominated screen script. But Lumet made a serious tactical error. By simulating in a horrific and bloody fashion the blinding of real horses, he outraged animal-lovers and shocked moviegoers. Animal-rights activists demonstrated against the movie, and as a consequence the film adaptation never gained wide distribution. Movie critics have recognised powerful qualities in the film, and both leads – Burton and Firth – received Oscar nominations along with Shaffer. All the same, Shaffer has remained implacably critical of the film, claiming that Lumet's cinematic approach to the story is far too literal to sustain the more abstract scenes.[1]

But, as for the stage play, reviewers joined audiences in lauding *Equus*. British reviewers called it vivid theatre

(Michael Billington, *Manchester Guardian*) evidencing dramatic techniques of the highest order (John Barber, *Daily Telegraph*). Harold Hobson, in the *Sunday Times*, called *Equus* 'a moving and deeply profound play'. Most American critics concurred. Thou h offering minor quibbles, Harold Clurman thought *Equus* brilliantly crafted and compelling (*Nation*), a view shared by Marilyn Stasio in *Cue*. Writing for the *New York Times*, Clive Barnes declared *Equus* to be enthralling, while Walter Kerr called it remarkable. For both Barnes and Kerr, Shaffer represented a new hope for Broadway. The play's stupendous theatricality was often mentioned (for instance, by Howard Kissel in *Women's Wear Daily*); Brendan Gill (*New Yorker*) found it ingenious and thrilling; Douglas Watt (*New York Sunday News*) thought it powerful and exciting; and Jack Kroll of *Newsweek* claimed that *Equus* represented pure theatre at its best. Given both critical and popular acclaim, *Equus* not surprisingly earned numerous major honours. Among them were the Outer Critics Circle Award for best play of the year (1975), the New York Drama Critics Circle Best Play Award of the 1974–5 season, the Antoinette Perry (Tony) Award for the best play of 1974–5 and the Los Angeles Drama Critics Award for best drama.[2]

Reasons for the play's impressive popularity are several. The author seizes upon a highly unusual sexual rite of passage, and structures his story using flashback scenes mediated by an omniscient narrator. A similar fused dramatic and narrative technique worked with some success in *Royal Hunt*. But it was with *Equus* that Shaffer's evolving theatrical methods first completely succeeded. For one thing, in *Equus* there is a deft balance between the outer narrative framework and the enacted interior scenes. It is the same pattern as Shaffer employs

in later dramas such as *Amadeus* and *Yonadab*. Shaffer
thereby both dramatises his story directly and comments
on the action through rationalising mediators. Well worth
noting too is the playwright's grounding in detective
mysteries, a background that becomes apparent as the
unusual story shuttles through time and space, uncovering
evidence in what is essentially a 'whodunit'. The
detective-story pattern shares features with classical
Greek drama in that both first establish a puzzle and then
methodically fill in the facts needed to resolve it. *Equus*
also embodies strong ritualistic elements during Alan
Strang's worship scenes, and the drama clearly does
concern problems in religious belief. Moreover, the play's
conclusion suggests that there are indeed non-rational
universal forces of great urgency that shape our lives.
Shaffer had timeless ritualised drama in mind when writing *Equus*, as suggested by his remarks in the Preface to
the *Collected Plays*. There he acknowledges, 'The image
of a human sacrifice . . . was intended' (p. xv). So *Equus*
would seem to have elements in common with ancient
Greek drama.

But on the surface level the plot of *Equus* more
obviously resembles a conventional criminal investigation.
The sleuthing physician asks *what* Alan Strang did, *why* he
did it, and *what* society can – or should – do about his
actions. On a second level Alan's problems are shown to
have affinities with those of Martin Dysart, society's agent
paid to rid it of irregularities in its citizens' behaviour. As
he delves into the psyche of his patient, the 'healer' loses
faith in his own role. Gradually, he comes to appreciate
and even approve of the boy's aberrant acts. Dysart
discovers what Strang can only intuitively sense, that the
boy's actions constitute a primitive form of religious
worship. Solving the boy's quandary by exorcising his

perverted worship of a horse god only compounds the dilemma for Dysart. *Equus* concludes with Dysart's own life hopelessly stalemated. He can neither create his own godhead nor live with his conscience in a hypocritical, godless society. Shaffer does not resolve the drama's central question but only explores the price sometimes exacted to achieve 'normality' – namely, the excision of what is unique in a person's character.[3]

Suspense grows from the beginning. Martin Dysart, a psychiatrist specialising in children, addresses the audience directly to explain a crisis that a unique patient has precipitated in his personal and professional life. Dysart's opening monologue establishes the drama's outer narrative framework. Throughout the play action is frozen when Dysart, as guide and mediator, comments to the audience on events in the story. At other times he slips smoothly into the action as a key player. His first lines are delivered from his darkened hospital office. Shaffer, however, brings into view the two other central protagonists via a flash forward. In the background is a living tableau of a teenaged lad nuzzling a horse figure (actually an actor wearing a stylised horse head). Pointing to the pair, Dysart remarks that the horse, not the boy, holds the key to Dysart's own dilemma: 'I'm lost . . . I'm desperate . . . In a way, it has nothing to do with this boy. The doubts have been there for years . . .' (p. 402).[4] Thus from the outset Shaffer establishes the purview of the play, in which the lives of these three figures – the ailing boy, the physician who is supposed to heal him and the mysterious horse deity – interlock.

Following his prologue, Dysart, Prospero- like, visually conjures up past events. The enacted story commences a few months earlier, with Hesther Salomon, magistrate of a children's court, entering in a state of high anxiety. She is distraught because Alan Strang, a local youth, has committed a 'crime' which represents, in her words, 'the most shocking case I ever tried' (p. 403). As society's agent of justice (her biblical surname is a clue) she is worried that Alan, who 'blinded six horses with a metal spike', cannot expect to receive fair treatment from the courts or the medical community for a deed so disgusting. Dysart reluctantly accepts the professional challenge posed by Hesther and takes on the case. At first Alan's manner disconcerts Dysart. The boy makes the therapist feel like the odd one out. Dysart explains to Hesther, 'He has the strangest stare I ever met . . . It's exactly like being accused. Violently accused. But of what?' (p. 408). The question of accusation is reinforced subconsciously when Dysart experiences nightmares in which he conducts ritualistic surgery on hundreds of children. Slitting them to remove their innards is a service to society, his medical peers claim in the dreams. But Dysart can no longer justify the procedure, and in the world of the nightmare he fears that he will himself become the victim if society becomes aware of his doubts. Through Dysart's dream, Shaffer implies an unspecified connection between the problems of patient and therapist. Individual rights and communal good conflict head-on, as the plot eventually makes clear.

Characterists of the detective story pervade the drama. The crime is known at the outset, but so too is the perpetrator. Left to be solved is the motivation. Dysart assumes the role of detective, his psychiatric skills serving as a key to Alan's unconscious. He discovers that the boy's parents have radically contradictory attitudes toward child-raising. At the heart of their differences are matters of religion and sex. Alan's schoolteacher mother, Dora, seeks to rear her son in accordance with an idealised, purified Christianity; Frank, the father, is agnostic, with beliefs stemming from a type of secular socialism. As a result of his parents' divergent attitudes, Alan initiates a personal religion symbolised by an icon that once dominated his bedroom. This picture showed Christ, bloodied and agonised, being led to crucifixion in chains. Frank tells Dysart that he eventually tore down the picture, and that the destruction of his private icon traumatised Alan. Only a substitute picture could placate the troubled youth: this time a picture of a white horse, bloody and writhing in pain, with huge accusing eyes. Frank suspects a distorted connection between Alan's sexual and religious natures:

> A boy spends night after night having this stuff read into him; an innocent man tortured to death – thorns driven into his head – nails into his hands – a spear jammed through his ribs. It can mark anyone for life, that kind of thing. I'm not joking. The boy was absolutely fascinated by all that. He was always mooning over religious pictures. I mean real kinky ones, if you receive my meaning. (p. 415)

Discounting his wife's intensive indoctrination of Alan in romanticised religion, the father advises Dysart, 'All that stuff to me is just bad sex.' Dora inadvertently confirms Frank's suspicions when describing for Dysart her convictions about sex – views that she communicated to Alan. For her, physical sex *per se* is unclean; genuine love must touch the soul:

> I told him the biological facts. But I also told him what I believed. That sex is not *just* a biological matter, but spiritual as well. That if God willed, he would fall in

96

love one day. That his task was to prepare himself for the most important happening of his life. And after that, if he was lucky, he might come to know a higher love still. (p. 415)

The psychiatrist detects the shadowy presence of horses in the mystery surrounding Alan. Using a game of question and answer with the lad, he learns of Alan's first horseback ride, at the age of six. The boy's account underscores how momentous the experience was. His senses of touch, smell, sight and hearing were so excited during the ride that, recollecting the effect on his impressionable psyche, he sums it up as 'sexy'. The gallop ended traumatically, however, when his father pulled him off the animal because he considered horses to be dangerous. In Alan's mind those incipient sexual sensations became fused with a sense of danger and the forbidden. The tripartite connection of sex, religious worship and horses was further solidified when Jill, who works at the local stables, found Alan a job there too. It was with Jill, in those stables, that Alan failed in his initial attempts at love-making.

The horse-for-God transference complicates but does not obscure the plot. Alan's 'crime' was a rite of passage gone awry. Dysart's professional task is to excise the boy's unique brand of horse worship, replacing it with socially acceptable behaviour. Alan will then no longer be traumatised by his 'god Equus' (*equus*, Latin for horse) and be able to pursue a 'normal' life. Herein lies the conflict for the doctor, in what is the second theme of *Equus*. Dysart's nightmare mirrors his own subversive judgement of the psychiatrist's trade. He comes to reject the official job description assigned him to remove a patient's aberrant behaviour. The ultimate goal of organised society is to

sustain the Normal. Dysart informs us at the beginning of
the play that he has lost faith in the doctrine of normality
and thus balks at applying a psychological scalpel to Alan.
During scene 18 of the first act he expresses his doubts to
Hesther; but she, as a representative of the Establishment, cannot see beyond the need to make Alan 'normal'.
For her, Dysart has a 'duty' to 'restore' the lad to 'a
normal life'. Partially though not totally convinced, the
doctor continues his regimen. Alan is consequently led to
re-enact the ritual worship of his personal horse deity in a
stunning theatrical episode that closes the first act. Under
Dysart's coaxing, the boy relives (while acting out) the
entire ritual leading to a naked midnight horseback
ride – his unique form of worship. Confession, absolution
and communion have roles in Alan's ritual, culminating in
sanctified self-eroticism. From that re-enactment, Dysart
comes to appreciate the extraordinary sexual and religious
proportions of Alan's worship. It is a worship that, before
the blinding of the horses, satisfied the needs of the
confused adolescent. Dysart now fears that the cure may
be more dangerous than the illness.

Society as a whole, however, has no such qualms. It is
exactly Alan's unapproved worship which officialdom
wants eliminated. In the second act, Dysart expresses to
Hesther his haunting reservations about Alan:

Can you think of anything worse one can do to anybody
than take away their worship? . . . I only know it's the
core of his life. What else has he got? Think about
him . . . He's a modern citizen for whom society
doesn't exist. He lives *one hour* every three
weeks – howling in a mist. And after the service kneels

to a slave who stands over him obviously and unthrow-
ably his master. With my body I thee worship!

(pp. 453–4)

Yet Hesther Salomon sees only the boy's agony in being
alienated from society. For her, as for society generally,
the solution is simple: remove Alan's pain. Her answer
circumscribes Dysart's own dilemma as well. Alan Strang
and Martin Dysart comprise two halves of the same
puzzle. Alan's independent conduct is unacceptable to
society. Dysart's professional obligations on behalf of the
state are no longer credible to him. Interlocked
psychically, neither protagonist faces a fulfilling future.

Equus in the final analysis centres on Dysart. Shaffer
shapes the doctor into a modern Everyman, the
enlightened contemporary citizen trapped by his culture
to pursue values in which he has no further faith. Dysart
assesses his own life coolly and clinically as befits a man of
science. But what he finds is someone bereft of 'human'
sensations – all intellect with no emotions. It is a state he
equates with the absence of worship. He considers his case
desperate because, unlike Alan, he has found no adequate
object to worship. He insists to Hesther, 'Without worship
you shrink, it's as brutal as that . . . I shrank my *own* life.
No one can do it for you. I settled for being pallid and
provincial, out of my own eternal timidity' (p. 455). Alan,
on the other hand, through worship has come to know a
passion unimaginable to Dysart. The detached healer of
men's minds finally understands Alan Strang's enigmatic
but alarming glare at their first meeting. He explains his
discovery to Hesther: 'But that boy has known a passion
more ferocious than I have felt in any second of my life.
And let me tell you something: I envy it . . . Don't you

see? That's the Accusation? That's what his stare has been saying to me all this time: "*At least I galloped! When did you?*" ' (p. 454)

'Professional' to the end, Dysart succumbs, subordinating his instincts to leave Alan uncured by society's standards. He will eradicate through psychological exorcism the worship that dominated the boy's life. The suspenseful drama ends using powerful images of Alan, under Dysart's direction, abreacting to the mutilation of the horses. Just as the psychiatrist suspected, Alan's blinding of the horses tied in with his failed attempts to make love to Jill. During the re-enactment, Dysart perceives (as we do) how closely integrated religious and sexual ecstasies are for Alan. Previously Equus had satisfied Alan's needs, spiritually as object of worship and physiologically as prompter of sexual release during his devised ritual. Jill became a rival of Equus, because she could provide Alan with a 'normal' expression of sexuality. The natural sound of horses scraping their hoofs while he tried to make love to Jill seemed proof to Alan that he was being watched by Equus and convicted of sacrilege. Thwarted in his attempts to make love 'normally', he rededicated his loyalty to Equus and chased away the girl – but to no avail. Equus's was an inflexible doctrine, implacable and unforgiving. Alan snapped when Equus direly threatened, 'The Lord thy God is a Jealous God. He sees you. He sees you forever and ever, Alan. He sees you! . . . He *sees you*!' (p. 474). Eyes and seeing are motifs that Shaffer underscores throughout the play, providing a thematic justification of Alan's 'crime'.

No longer willing to be watched and monitored by judgemental figures, Alan exploded. He rejected the horse god's ultimatum, shouting, 'Thou – God – Seest –

NOTHING!' (p. 474). With that, he seized a hoof pick and struck out the eyes of six horses that had 'witnessed' his unsuccessful act of love. According to society's rationale, upon eradicating the traumatic deed through psychological cleansing, Alan should be freed from his obsession with Equus. But, for both the patient and physician, the matter is not so tidy. The play's final scene shows Dysart still grimly dubious. He admits to the exhausted, unconscious boy that his god may or may not vanish: 'He won't really go that easily . . . Oh no! When Equus leaves – if he leaves at all – it will be with your intestines in his teeth. And I don't stock replacements . . . If you knew anything, you'd get up this minute and run from me fast as you could' (p. 475).

Although he accepts responsibility for destroying Alan's intuitive worship, Dysart is dismayed by the dilemma which as a consequence becomes his own. Now he assumes the moral burdens sparked by Alan's creation of Equus-as-God. The play concludes with a parallel tableau to the one that opens the play, only this time it is the physician who is being tyrannised by the horse deity locked into his brain. Hopelessness permeates Dysart's closing lines: 'And now for me it never stops: that voice of Equus out of the cave – "Why Me? . . . Why Me? . . . Account for Me!" . . . There is now, in my mouth, this sharp chain. And it never comes out' (p. 476).

Thematically, *Equus* gains effectiveness from the skilful manner in which Alan's burgeoning sexuality is integrated with his personally defined religion. Simultaneously, Shaffer dramatises Dysart's worsening personal situation as the obverse of the boy's condition. Alan the adolescent discovers the power of sexual energy; Dysart at middle age no longer touches his wife. More significantly, the ignorant lad constructs his own primitive system of deities, while the highly educated physician flounders in a barren spiritual landscape.

Shaffer's composite characterisation of Alan and Dysart constitutes a remarkable vehicle by which to explore their interlocked fates. As each piece of Alan's story falls into place, a new facet of the doctor is also exposed. Take for example the contrast between them in terms of sexuality. Alan's first horseback ride was also the first time he felt the stirrings of sexual arousal, as his description of it makes clear: 'I was pushed forward on the horse. There was sweat on my legs from his neck. The fellow held me tight, and let me turn the horse which way I wanted. All the power going any way you wanted . . .' (p. 426). Moreover, Jill's instructions to Alan for brushing a horse's coat are scarcely veiled descriptions of foreplay: 'Now you always groom the same way . . . Don't be afraid to do it hard. The harder you do it, the more the horse loves it. Push it right through the coat: like this' (p. 443). These and similar allusions point the way to Alan's unique rites, involving a comprehensive sexual experience. This is obvious from his description of his worship of Equus, which begins with touching the horse 'All over. Everywhere', and concludes with his own cries at climax:

Feel me on you! *On* you! *On* you! *On* you!
I want to be *in* you!
Equus, I love you! . . .
Make us One Person!   (p. 448)

Alan's awakening sexuality is counterbalanced by Dysart's loss of passion, sexual or otherwise. It is a loss the disillusioned doctor fully comprehends, and he ironically compares his relationship with Margaret, his wife, to Alan's passion: 'I watch that woman knitting, night after night – a woman I haven't *kissed* in six years – and he stands in the dark for an hour, sucking the sweat off his God's hairy cheek!' (p. 455).

For many playgoers, however, the ultimate achievement of *Equus* lies in its brilliant theatricality, not its melodrama. From the outset, Shaffer acknowledged an immense debt to director John Dexter for developing the final staging of the work.[5] The result was a presentation of spartan simplicity that allowed the audience plenty of scope to visualise the unfolding episodes. The set is described as a '*square of wood set on a circle of wood*', with the innermost square resembling '*a railed boxing ring*'. The pugilistic allusion is apt. The centre stage functions subtextually as an arena in which a vigorous contest for control of modern man's soul is fought out. Though its trappings and surface story differ markedly from those of his other major works, *Equus* picks up one of Shaffer's central concerns, the ongoing struggle between conformity and individuality. Or, in Shaffer's own choice of terms, it is Dionysian self-expression pitted against Apollonian self-control.[6] Given that combat, a sports arena makes perfect sense as *mise en scène*. Shaffer's stage directions also suggest that the play area should resemble a surgical amphitheatre where a clinical dissection will take place. Rows of curved benches, following the contour of the stage circle, envelop the brightly illuminated acting space on three sides. The on-stage audience witnesses the psychological analyses or dissections close at hand.[7]

The flexibility of the stage design permits striking variations in the way the action is presented. Straightforward realism alternates with imaginative stylised scenes of mime. Dysart's is the cool, detached world of science where clinical evidence determines one's actions. His dealings with others are consequently portrayed realistically, with narrated interjections. But Alan Strang's ritual worship is especially well suited to abstract staging. During such scenes Shaffer radically shifts tone through masks, lighting changes and sound effects. Symbols and mimed rituals dominate. Essential to the plot and most memorable of the abstractions are the horses devised for *Equus*. They must evoke the essence of horses as we recognise them in daily life, but should also have the regal bearing of transcendent beings as Alan perceived them. Shaffer, with the advice of John Dexter, elected to have actors play the horse roles in wholly non-realistic fashion. The published stage directions are clear: '*Any literalism which could suggest the cosy familiarity of a domestic animal – or worse, a pantomime horse – should be avoided.*' Actors portraying the horses typically wear dark velvet tracksuits with matching gloves, and masks made of light metal and leather strips. Again, realistic depiction is to be avoided: '*The actors' own heads are seen beneath them*; *no attempt should be made to conceal them.*' The same actors wear raised metal footgear reminiscent of the *kothornoi* worn in ancient Greek theatre. The actors are to stand upright at all times, and any animal effects '*must be created entirely mimetically*'. Even donning the horse masks on stage must aim for '*an exact and ceremonial effect*'.

John Dexter's seminal part in realising Shaffer's script cannot be overestimated. He and Shaffer concurred that *Equus* required a totally committed collaboration. Shaffer openly admits his debt to Dexter, writing, 'The power of the play seemed to be constantly inside me, telling me where to go with it. I think the director would agree that it largely told him also. The excellence of Dexter's achievement lay in controlling that power – avoiding from the beginning to end the slightest sense of absurdity, which can easily arise when actors perform as animals . . .' (Preface, p. xv). Dexter in a 1979 interview insisted on exactly the same point, saying about the effort of *Equus*, 'That's what we're there to do – struggle. I don't think a director arrives with conclusions. A broad response to the play, a designer with whom you have total sympathy and understanding, and then everybody trusts each other from there on. Ideas are thrown around and around, and everything's a collaboration.'[8]

The parameters designated by the playtext are explicit and demanding. Shaffer warns against attempts to replicate horse whinnying, for instance. The horse actors, who for much of the time sit on benches up-stage, are to create a choric effect by '*humming, thumping, and stamping*' to announce each appearance of Equus the God. During flashback episodes, the lights turn warm in colour and intensity, investing the remembered action with a patina of memory glow. Lighting effects are most obvious in remembered scenes such as that of Alan's first horse ride, and when Jill is on stage. Through such technical means Shaffer carefully guides the audience between the competing realms of realistic and high stylised narrative.

With *Equus*, Peter Shaffer's dramatic techniques lead to a more focused outcome. He chooses a contemporary cultural concern for his surface plot: namely, the trade-off between the Dionysian and Apollonian elements present in all humans. We have witnessed the collision of these impulses before in Shaffer's dramas. In *Equus* the problem is to reconcile the conflicting demands of individual will and society's requirements. Beneath the social dimension, however, lies Shaffer's pre-eminent subject: our eternal search for a deity who can lend meaning to our mortal existence. When *Equus* first appeared, in the

1970s, Shaffer's concern for metaphysical absolutes was in tune with the mainstream existentialism then dominating intellectual thought. However, the play displays strong staying powers, whatever the specific historical or cultural context, because an examination of man's relationship to his god remains valid – and urgent – in any era.

What will be best remembered about *Equus* is its brilliant dramatising of man's attempt to reconcile the personal and the metaphysical aspects of his universe. With John Dexter's immeasurable help, Shaffer strikingly fused realism with mimetic ritual. And the daring stylisation so prominent in *Equus* is matched by the daring use of human nudity and animal mutilation – neither of which would fit within a realistic framework. The occasional rhetorical bluster of *Royal Hunt* is averted here for the most part, and the stylised episodes of *Equus* are kept in tight control, calling less attention to themselves than do the mimed scenes of the earlier work. Then, too, Peter Shaffer's natural proclivity for the mystery and suspense of the whodunit serves him well in *Equus*, where a deep psychological puzzle is investigated until its secrets are brought to light. Taken on its own terms, *Equus* stands as one of the finest suspense dramas of our time.

6
'Amadeus': Shaffer's Supreme Achievement

Amadeus is Peter Shaffer's most accomplished and successful drama to date. Starting from a tantalising rumour regarding the untimely death of Wolfgang Amadeus Mozart in 1791, Shaffer fashions an absorbing costume spectacle built on ambition, aesthetics, politics and metaphysics. During the final weeks of his life, an ailing and destitute Mozart claimed aloud that he was being poisoned by Antonic Salieri, court composer to Emperor Joseph II and, at the time, more successful than Mozart. The story erupted again thirty years later when an aged and deranged Salieri confessed in writing to having killed Mozart. And then, lending still more credence to the gossip, Salieri unsuccessfully tried to take his own life. Artists before Shaffer – Pushkin and Rimsky-Korsakov, among others – had drawn on the dubious murder theory,[1] but Shaffer's approach to the mystery is unique, because *Amadeus* moves well beyond a simple dramatisation of the juicy gossip. The competitive antagonisms between the two musical figures are reconfigured into a metaphysical enigma. Moreover, Shaffer's design approaches the themes imaginatively from an unlikely perspective by centring *Amadeus* on Salieri, not Mozart.

Fascinated by Salieri's alleged confessions, Shaffer found some noteworthy paradoxes when researching the historical and biographical sources. An ideal dramatic situation began to present itself. Salieri and Mozart followed contrasting careers in Joseph II's Austria. Historical accounts revealed that Antonio Salieri, a sophisticated and pious man with impeccable musical credentials, enjoyed material bounty throughout his career. A 'team player', he never strayed from the established social and musical mores of the court, providing precisely the middle-of-the-road compositions demanded by the emperor. Appointed to progressively higher posts in Viennese musical circles, he came to be seen as possibly the foremost composer of the day. The infinitely more talented Mozart, conversely, had far less success in career terms, though he did not go without recognition. Only seventy of his 626 compositions were published during his short lifetime. High-spirited and determinedly independent in temperament, the prodigy from Salzburg boldly disregarded the well-defined rules of conduct prevailing in Viennese court society. All the evidence points to an obvious genius filled with personal ambition and a keen desire for professional success. But Mozart also seemed unwilling (or unable) to tone down his independence and originality to curry favour with the Establishment. Shaffer's authoritative sources furnished profuse material for shaping a dramatic portrait of Mozart. Less verifiable, historically, is Shaffer's characterisation of Salieri, whose life story was altered for dramaturgical purposes. In defence of the dramatist it must be stressed that he never claimed to have produced a historically accurate portrait of either composer. Nor does he deplore Salieri's musical accomplishments in the abstract. It is when the two composers' works are compared from today's perspective that the Italian comes off a weak second best.

Shaffer was struck by the fact that the stupendous genius of Mozart could not secure him a successful life and career, whereas the lesser talent of Salieri was rewarded with the highest accolades that his contemporaries could offer. He thus enjoyed higher respect and a more comfortable life than Mozart. Yet Mozart was the eventual winner, in that he has long been recognised as one of the world's greatest composers, while Salieri has been generally forgotten. Few other than musicologists had even heard of him when *Amadeus* placed him back in the spotlight. Shaffer believed that the more intriguing vantage point resided with the lesser man, Salieri, whose situation corresponds with that of ordinary persons – those who, like him lead a life in accordance with the 'standard' values of their time. Salieri's plight manifests our own, raising the metaphysical riddles that haunt all Shaffer's serious dramas. In particular, he seeks to fathom the universal design of a god so unjust to his human creation.

Opening in November 1979 at the National Theatre in London, with Paul Scofield as Salieri in a production directed by Peter Hall, *Amadeus* won London's major drama prizes and enjoyed a lengthy run. Shaffer recognised certain weaknesses in the script and continued to make revisions during the early months of 1980. A revised, tightened version opened at the National Theatre, Washington, that November. A month later *Amadeus* moved to Broadway's Broadhurst Theatre, where it became the hit of the season, eventually winning five Tony Awards including Best Play. Milos Forman's 1984 film adaptation also gained great critical and popular acclaim, securing eight Academy Awards, including Best Picture, Best Actor and Best Screenplay (written by Shaffer).[2] Moreover, the movie soundtrack – carefully assembled from Mozart's compositions by Shaffer, Forman and musical director Neville Marriner – became a bestseller in the classical music charts.[3] When the dust settled, *Amadeus* had expanded beyond a stage hit into the most talked about cultural phenomenon of the early 1980s.

Media critics responded to *Amadeus* with an enthusiasm matching that of the general public. Steve Grant of the *Observer* (11 November 1979) described the play as a 'marvellously engrossing and moving costume-thriller, a feast for the eye and the ear'. Frank Rich in the *New York Times* (18 December 1980) judged the Broadway version a 'triumphant production' that 'fills the theatre with that mocking, heavenly silence that is the overwhelming terror of life'. Many reviewers acknowledged provocative ideas in the play. Bernard Levin in *The Times* (2 December 1979) urged audiences to keep an open mind, because 'those who go to it prepared to understand what it is about will have an experience that far transcends even its considerable value as drama'. Edwin Wilson in the *Wall Street Journal* (19 December 1980) noted that *Amadeus* probes serious questions 'in a most original way and thereby provides the most ingenious and engrossing theatre piece we have seen in some time'.

At the same time, Shaffer struck a sensitive nerve. There was an element of notoriety in the play's celebrity. The very innovativeness in Shaffer's handling of the story became a major source of complaint. For his dramatic design to work, the playwright had to provide an unflinchingly accurate portrait of Mozart. Shaffer's Mozart, based on authoritative sources, stepped on stage as foulmouthed, childish, irresponsible and impossibly arrogant.[4] Shaffer immeasurably heightened the play's interest by exposing the less idealised, more human qualities in Mozart's nature. But he also aroused the ire of some commentators and almost all musicologists.[5] For Mozart purists, *Amadeus* was sacrilegious and scurrilous for depicting a supreme prodigy as a ruffian. For other music enthusiasts, Mozart could never again be considered as simplistically as before.

Yet Shaffer's focus is not on Mozart, and critics claiming *Amadeus* to be an attack on the composer are misguided. Mozart's music is nowhere denigrated in the play, nor is Mozart made a villain. *Amadeus* instead fictionalises the story of Antonio Salieri's aspirations, with Mozart limited to playing the lesser composer's foil and antagonist. Shaffer understood how crucial it was to create a proper balance between his main characters, leading him to revise the text before its American production. In the Preface to the *Collected Plays* he explains, 'One of the faults which I believe existed in the London version was simply that Salieri had too little to do with Mozart's ruin . . . Now, in this new American version, he [Salieri] stands where he properly belongs – at the wicked centre of the action' (p. xvii).[6] Either Mozart's or Salieri's personality could on its own command audience interest. But Shaffer deftly draws on documentary material to weave together their lives and careers into an engrossing whole.

Beneath the surface skirmishes between Mozart and Salieri, Shaffer sensed a raging combat to do with matters of greater consequence than mere earthly reputation. At the core of *Amadeus* lies his concern about the bewildering relationship between man and God. Like most believers, the Salieri of the play seeks a rapprochement with the ruling deity of his universe. In his unique way, he 'hunts' for a reliable and fair god as do Pizarro in *Royal Hunt* and Dysart in *Equus*. Without confidence in the ultimate orderliness of the universe there can be no faith in human institutions, a condition mirrored in contemporary man's spiritual malaise. Salieri is typical of Shaffer's protagonists in that he eventually finds himself betrayed by a god he thought knowable and trustworthy. He becomes an Everyman, one of us, trying to ascertain reliable rules by which to conduct his life. The Mozart of the play is therefore less important as a historical character than as proof to Salieri of God's unreliability. But, unlike Pizarro and Dysart, Salieri does not merely bemoan his disappointment with an incomprehensible god. In fury and frustration, he challenges God to do battle, insisting that human beings need not tolerate inadequate deities. Part of the strength of *Amadeus* lies in the way Shaffer steps up his treatment of the man–God relationship. Man here declares outright war on what he perceives as faulty universal powers.

Amadeus is Peter Shaffer's finest attempt to explore abstract metaphysical concerns, but never loses sight of the human dimensions of the story he tells. He arouses audience curiosity by turning Mozart's alleged murder into an irresistible mystery which we are invited to help solve. Early in the play Salieri puts the matter thus: '*The Death of Mozart, – or, Did I Do It?*' *Amadeus* is thus cast as a detective story in which relevant details regarding real persons and real historical facts must be found to answer Salieri's teasing question to the audience. In the search for evidence and answers, the play exposes unsettling, even shocking, factors regarding Mozart's life and times. Shaffer's eighteenth-century Vienna is dominated by personal and political intrigue, sex, jealousy, alleged murder and attempted suicide. We see all the sordid details through Salieri, who in Shaffer's structure becomes the lens for all events. To present 'evidence' concerning the mystery, Salieri requires freedom to move through space and time. Shaffer masterfully accommodates that need by circumscribing events with an outer narrative frame comparable to those in *The Royal Hunt of the Sun* and *Equus*. Salieri thereby gains flexible narrative options. Free from the tyranny of plot illusion, he enjoys full access to the audience. As narrator, he can provide vital exposition directly. Even as participant in enacted events, he can voice subconscious thoughts by momentarily freezing actions to address us in asides. There is a further advantage in the drama's adaptable narrative design: by addressing the audience so often and so intimately, Salieri not only makes playgoers witness to the proceedings but systematically draws them into a form of complicity.

Amadeus opens with a very old Salieri sitting alone, in a wheelchair. Overheard in the background are hissed whisperings of Salieri's name fused with the word 'assassin'. The voices belong to the Venticelli, Salieri's 'little winds'. Like wind instruments, the Venticelli express themselves in a musical manner, at times in stichomythic patter talk and sometimes in choral unison. Structurally, they are ironic chorus as well as Salieri's spies within the inner story. The scene is set in 1823, long after Mozart's death. But Salieri, an antique relic from the glorious years of Joseph II, remains obsessed with Mozart. After repeating in Italian that he repents having killed Mozart, Salieri abruptly turns to address the audience. He calls them the Ghosts of the Future and asks them to 'be my Confessors!'

(p. 487). The old man has something to confess concerning Mozart, and the audience has power of absolution. Salieri follows with a spellbinding monologue in which he tells about his upbringing and early career. We learn that a single-minded passion ruled his youth: to become famous as a musician and composer.

The urgency of Salieri's early ambition is underscored by his admission. 'I wanted Fame. Not to deceive you. I wanted to *blaze*, like a comet, across the firmament of Europe. Yet only in one especial way. Music' (p. 488). So intense was his drive for celebrity that as a youth Salieri proposed a Faustian pact with God. The elderly Salieri figure repeats his youthful vows to a god once thought trustworthy: '*Signore*, let me be a Composer! Grant me sufficient fame to enjoy it. In return I will live with virtue. I will be chaste. I will strive to better the lot of my fellows. And I will honour You with much music all the days of my life!' (p. 489). Salieri's bargain with God is apparently honoured and success immediately follows. But doubts arise when Wolfgang Amadeus Mozart arrives to threaten Salieri's superiority in Vienna's musical hierarchy. For the first time Salieri, the Establishment court composer, feels anxiety. Suddenly, in a brilliant *coup de théâtre*, the aged Salieri figure wheels around, shedding his robe and sleeping cap to reveal a youthful persona from forty years earlier. The story thereafter proceeds chronologically, dramatising moments from Salieri's middle career when Mozart was his chief rival. Through a blend of enacted episodes and direct asides, we trace Salieri's life and frustrated aspirations – all of which lead to the alleged assassination. Aside from a brief appearance to conclude the opening act, the aged Salieri does not return until the final moments of *Amadeus*. Most of the remainder of the play focuses on the life and times of Antonio Salieri – which also happen to involve Mozart.

Act I of *Amadeus* sets out the happy circumstances of Salieri's early career. Speaking directly to the audience, the composer expresses satisfaction with his life and with a world readily understood and simple to deal with. His immediate goal in 1781 at the age of thirty-one is to attain the position of First Royal Kapellmeister, a post he will eventually achieve. He has set notions concerning the responsibilities of court musician and composer. He considers himself and other musicians 'servants' whose task is 'to celebrate men's average lives! . . . We took unremarkable men: usual bankers, run-of-the-mill priests, ordinary soldiers and statesmen and wives – and sacramentalized their mediocrity' (p. 490). Shaffer later marvellously contrasts Salieri's mundane view of music's function with Mozart's majestic theories. When pressed by his lacklustre musical colleagues, Mozart sets down his views on music:

> I bet that's how God hears the world. Millions of sounds ascending at once and mixing in His ear to become an unending music, unimaginable to us! [*To* SALIERI.] That's our job, we composers: to combine the inner minds of him and him, and her and her – the thoughts of chambermaids and Court Composers – and turn the audience into God.   (p. 527)

Word of Mozart's arrival in Vienna comes from the Venticelli, who speed to Salieri with their reports. At first Salieri remains unconcerned. He begins to feel uneasy when he meets the newcomer at an evening entertainment before an aristocratic audience. Shaffer concocts a splendid and effective scene in the library of the hostess,

Baroness Waldstädten, for Salieri's introduction to Mozart the man and to his music. First, the unseen Salieri overhears the childish patter of Mozart romping with his fiancée Constanze. Thinking they are alone, Mozart cat-like chases the girl around the library, sometimes on all fours: 'I'm going to pounce-bounce! I'm going to scrunch-munch! I'm going to chew-poo my little mouse-wouse! I'm going to tear her to bits with my paws-claws! . . . You're trembling! . . . I think you're frightened of puss-wuss . . . I think you're scared to death! [*Intimately.*] I think you're going to shit yourself' (p. 495). Thus Shaffer conveys one distasteful truth about Mozart's personality – his foul-mouthed coarseness, accompanied by a perpetual imma-turity of manner. Salieri, like the audience, is stunned. Yet, when he hears Mozart's music being played else-where in the palace, he is overwhelmed by a different shock:

> It started simply enough: just a pulse in the lowest registers – bassoons and basset horns – like a rusty squeezebox . . . And then suddenly, high above it, sounded a single note on the oboe. [*We hear it.*] It hung there unwavering – piercing me through – till breath could hold it no longer, and a clarinet withdrew it out of me, and sweetened it into a phrase of such delight it had me trembling. The light flickered in the room. My eyes clouded! . . . [*Calling up in agony.*]'*What?! What is this? Tell me, Signore!* What is this *pain*? What is this *need* in the sound? Forever unfulfillable yet fulfilling him who hears it, utterly! Is it *Your* need? . . . *Can it be Yours?*' . . . I was suddenly frightened. It seemed to me I had heard a voice of God – and that it issued from a creature whose own voice I had also heard – and it was the voice of an obscene child! (pp. 496–7)

Much of the remainder of the first act depicts Mozart's slow, laboured progress at the court of Joseph II. His musical genius is undeniable, but so too are his boorish manners and arrogant insults of his fellow composers. Very much the German chauvinist, he regularly snipes at the Italian influence in the imperial court, naming names in the process: 'Vienna is completely in the hands of foreigners. Worthless wops like *Kapellmeister Bonno*!' (p. 507). On such occasions, when he has been drinking too freely (as is often the case), Mozart complains openly about Salieri's uninspired music as well: 'Tonic and dominant, tonic and dominant from here to resurrection! Not one interesting modulation all night. Salieri is a musical idiot!' (p. 508). Mozart's published correspondence is a rich source of such anecdotes, including gibes at the emperor's tightfistedness; in *Amadeus* Mozart notes that 'behind his back His Majesty is known as Kaiser Keep It' (p. 508). All the while Salieri, now alert to the potential danger of his rival's enormous talent, keeps a wary eye on Mozart. Act I closes with a masterful theatrical scene in which Salieri '*greedily*' peruses original scores of Mozart's music that he has managed to wangle out of Constanze. The music sounds while he reads and ceases when he looks away. All his worst fears are realised, and yet he is sufficiently honest to acknowledge the significance of what he is hearing: 'I was staring through the cage of those meticulous ink strokes at an Absolute Beauty!' (p. 519), whereupon he falls into a faint.

Salieri's bargain with God is a failure, given what he has heard. In one of his renowned *coups de théâtre*, Shaffer puts in Salieri's mouth a renunciation of the earlier sacred pact. Addressing God, Salieri declares,

You gave me the desire to serve you – which most men do not have – then saw to it the service was shameful in the ears of the server. *Grazie!* You gave me the desire to praise you – which most do not feel – then made me mute. *Grazie tanti!* You put into me perception of the Incomparable – which most men never know! – then ensured that I would know myself forever mediocre. [*His voice gains power.*] *Why? . . . What is my fault? . . .* Until this day I have pursued virtue with rigor. I have labored long hours to relieve my fellow men. I have worked and worked the talent you allowed me . . . Solely that in the end, in the practice of the art which alone makes the world comprehensible to me, I might hear Your Voice! And now I do hear it – and it says only one name: MOZART! . . . Spiteful, sniggering, conceited, infantile Mozart! . . . – *him* you have chosen to be your sole conduct! And *my* only reward – my sublime privilege – is to be the sole man alive in this time who shall clearly recognize your incarnation! [*Savagely.*] *Grazie e grazie ancora!*

(pp. 519–20)

In fury and hubris, Antonio Salieri risks Christian damnation by flinging a challenge to a universal force which apparently ignores all rules of fairness:

From this time we are enemies, You and I! I'll not accept it from You. *Do you hear? . . .* They say God is not mocked. I tell you, *Man* is not mocked! . . . *I* am not mocked! . . . *Dio Inguisto!* You are the Enemy! . . . I name Thee now – *Nemico Eterno!* And this I swear. To my last breath I shall *block* you on earth, as far as I am able! (p. 520)

Salieri's complete disillusionment reflects a common human reaction when an agreement made in good faith is violated by one of the parties involved. Salieri had laid out the exact terms of the initial bargain with a god whom he considered reliable and he had kept his word till that point. But, when the amoral, irreligious and brutish Mozart becomes God's musical conduit on earth, Salieri sees himself betrayed. The character of Salieri corresponds to Pizarro in *Royal Hunt* and Dysart in *Equus*. All three Apollonian characters abide by behavioural conventions defined by their respective societies, and, as a consequence, all find their lives constricted and unfulfilled. Mozart in turn matches Dionysian personalities such as Atahuallpa and Alan Strang. Each follows an anarchistic, disruptive path which violates standard societal strictures. They are guided by their own intuitions. In each case, the eccentric conduct of the Dionysian figures brings condemnation from society at large. Apollonian personalities, however, who value order and predictability, gain community approval, though often at the cost of personal disappointment with their lives. Regarding the Apollonian – Dionysian struggle, Shaffer admits that 'I just feel in myself that there is a constant debate going on between the violence of instinct on the one hand and the desire in my mind for order and restraint . . .'[7]

One significant difference separates Antonio Salieri from Shaffer's previous Apollonian protagonists, and it is that change which transforms *Amadeus* into a more comprehensive dramatic fable. Pizarro and Dysart, previous Apollonians, envied Atahuallpa and Alan Strang, the Dionysians, for the supreme individuality they have achieved by flouting conventional standards. Salieri, though admitting Mozart's superior musical ability, in no way wishes to 'become' his antagonist (Pizarro physically binds himself to Atahuallpa, and Dysart confesses his envy of Alan). Quite the opposite: Salieri sees Mozart as an aberration in the universal order, and thus as something that must be destroyed. Instead of considering Mozart's superiority evidence that *no* deity controls the world, Salieri arrogantly interprets Mozart's genius a personal insult from a cruel, dishonest god. He must therefore retaliate for the damage to his personal honour – and to that of mankind. A diatribe that he hurls against God in Act I concludes with mocking words, 'What use, after all, is Man, if not to teach God His Lessons?' (p. 520).

Amadeus eventually answers the question regarding Mozart's death. Act I, as we have seen, focuses on Salieri's original bargain with God and his growing conviction that Mozart's extraordinary talent represents God's betrayal of the agreement. But, with the extension of Shaffer's Apollonian–Dionysian theories, Act II assumes a distinct function of its own: that of clarifying Salieri's relationship to Mozart. At the beginning of the act Salieri '*comes downstage and addresses the Audience directly*' to announce a new-found goal after discovering God's treachery: 'On that dreadful night of the manuscripts my life acquired a terrible and thrilling purpose. The blocking of God in one of his purest manifestations. I had the power. God needed Mozart to let himself into the world. And Mozart needed *me* to get him worldly advancement. So it would be a battle to the end – and Mozart was the battleground' (p. 521). The second act of *Amadeus* therefore chronicles Salieri's new campaign, one aimed not at winning God's approval but at striking back. A new element of suspense is introduced too, since Salieri's aim is nothing less than to harrow God. How will God react to Salieri's attack on his chosen musical vessel on earth?

Salieri recognises the danger – 'Would He strike me dead for my impiety?' – and yet remains strangely excited. Here and throughout the drama he remains unrepentant and in fact comes to epitomise man's mean-mindedness. Salieri mockingly comments to his audience, 'God was a cunning Enemy. Witness the fact that in blocking Him in the world I was also given the satisfaction of obstructing a disliked human rival. I wonder which of you will refuse that chance if it is offered' (p. 521).

Irony dominates *Amadeus*, and God's response will not become evident until the end of the play. Meanwhile, Salieri leads to more harmful consequences for Mozart, and Salieri's own circumstances steadily improve. Like Iago, he turns to subtle intrigue, denying Mozart better-paying court posts and using all available means to limit the success of his rival's operas. Salieri pretends friendship to Mozart but offers ill advice that leads to disastrous results, as with the portrayal of Masonic rites in *The Magic Flute*.

Near the play's conclusion the audience finally receives answers about Mozart's death and Salieri's possible involvement. Part of the answer concerns a mysterious man wearing a large cape, arms outstretched as though to embrace an unseen other. It is that figure that became the visual emblem for *Amadeus* in promotional material. The different incarnations of the silhouetted form come together during Mozart's death scene. In Mozart's weakened mind, the mysterious figure blurs into separate but interconnected persons. One shape involves a messenger from a certain Count Walsegg who commissioned Mozart to write a requiem mass – a mass, in fact, that the eccentic nobleman later performed and claimed to have composed. This is the sole historically based variant of the figure. Another version was specifically conceived for the play: to harass his rival, Salieri takes to stalking outside Mozart's apartment, donning an oversized grey cloak like the one Mozart sees in his dreams. As such, the disguised Salieri becomes the '*Messenger of God*', warning Mozart of imminent death. Moreover, Shaffer had read authoritative accounts of Mozart's special attachment of his father Leopold, whose returned spirit is one of the identities assigned to the cloaked figure. And eventually the mysterious stranger is transformed into his father in the deranged mind of Mozart. On the verge of death and crazed by fever, Mozart cries out, 'Take me, Papa. Take me. Put down your arms and I'll hop into them' (p. 552).

Salieri admits hounding Mozart to death by denying him life, not by inflicting direct physical damage. At the play's climax, he reveals the full circumstances of the 'murder'. In a mock ritual, he tears off and eats a piece of musical manuscript, explaining to the dying Mozart, 'I eat what God gives me. Dose after dose. For all my life. His poison. We are both poisoned, Amadeus. I with you; you with me . . . *Ecco mi*. Antonio Salieri. Ten years of my hate have poisoned you to death . . . Die, Amadeus! Die, I beg you, die! . . . Leave me alone, *ti imploro*! Leave me alone at last!' (p. 552). Mozart in fact will die of physical ailments having nothing to do with poison, and Salieri's claim is that he has 'killed' Mozart by sabotaging his career whenever possible.

Salieri appears to have won his battle with God. Mozart lies dead, and Salieri goes on to experience a fame undimmed by more talented rivals. Irony, however, provides the prevailing tonality for *Amadeus*. No character is more attuned to that fact than Salieri, who is subjected to a triple dose before the play is over. First, he is drowned in a praise which he alone knows is misguided. Towards the end of the drama he has returned to his principal narrative role, speaking directly to the audience: 'And so I stayed on in the City of Musicians, reverenced by all! *On* and *on* and *on*! . . . *For thirty-two years*! . . . And slowly I understood the nature of God's punishment . . . I was to be bricked up in Fame! Buried in Fame! Embalmed in Fame! But for work I knew to be absolutely worthless!' (p. 556). A second wave of irony descends when Mozart's music becomes the rage of Europe. Though a celebrity, Salieri soon holds no musical interest for the Austrians. In Salieri's ironic perspective, 'I must survive to see myself become *extinct*!'

The action reverts to 1823 with an aged Salieri again presiding at the close of the play. He has one trick left to play in his continuing war with God. By convincing everyone that he did indeed poison Mozart to death, he means to retrieve at least one form of immortality, in spite of – and to spite – God. To clinch his niche in history, he intends to commit suicide. He elaborates for the audience:

> They will learn of my dreadful death – and they will believe the lie forever! After today, whenever men speak Mozart's name with love, they will speak mine with loathing! As his name grows in the world so will mine – if not in fame, then in infamy. *I'm going to be immortal after all*! And He is powerless to prevent it!
>
> (p. 557)

The third and most bitter dose of irony, however, is that Salieri does not succeed in taking his own life. Thereafter he lives entirely forgotten while Mozart's renown soars. Salieri's failed suicide aptly parallels his inability to destroy Mozart's monumental reputation during their rivalry in Vienna. Shaffer concludes *Amadeus* showing Salieri, decrepit and embittered, offering a sour benediction to the audience: 'Mediocrities everywhere – now and to come – I absolve you all. Amen!' (p. 558)

Never before had Shaffer so integrated his audience into the fabric of his drama. Narrators standing outside the action are common in his plays, appearing also in *Royal Hunt*, *Equus* and *Yonadab*. *Amadeus*, however, encourages the audience to participate, witnessing the events as Salieri outlines them, confessing then absolving him just as he ironically confesses and absolves his spectators. Shaffer tacitly aligns the audience with Salieri, who in his mediocrity represents the vast majority of ordinary people. Our pedestrian lives are led with no fanfare and little derring-do, and most of us hold pedestrian social and aesthetic values sanctioned by convention. Nowhere is leaden tradition more obvious than in the scenes concerning music. Salieri is archdeacon of musical conventionality in the drama, and he scoffs at Mozart's renowned 'Marten aller Arten' aria from *The Abduction from the Seraglio*, describing it as 'Ten minutes of scales and ornaments, amounting in sum to a vast emptiness' (p. 504). Count Rosenberg similarly complains about the opera, claiming that it possesses 'too many notes', a criticism repeated by Emperor Joseph in a comment verified by history (in *Amadeus* the line is, 'There are in fact only so many notes the ear can hear in the course of an evening' – p. 505).

Not only does Mozart openly criticise general musical standards in his day as dominated by 'tonic and dominant'; he expresses impatience with the operatic writing as well. His colleagues chide him for wanting to compose an opera based on Beaumarchais's notorious play *The Marriage of Figaro*. Shaffer's Mozart argues passionately for more vitality on the operatic stage. To Van Swieten he declares, 'I want to do a piece about real people, Baron! And I want to set it in a real place! A *Boudoir*! – because

that to me is the most exciting place on earth! Under-
clothes on the floor! Sheets still warm from a woman's body!
Even a pisspot brimming under the bed!' (p. 526). The
character of Mozart often voices sentiments expressing
the actual notions of his historical progenitor, thereby
infusing the play with intelligent musical insights. Another
instance arises when Mozart considers aloud the unique
advantages of the operatic medium: 'Astonishing device:
a vocal quartet! . . . I tell you I want to write a finale
lasting half an hour! a quartet becoming a quintet becoming a sextet. On and on, wider and wider – all sounds
multiplying and rising together – and then together making a sound entirely new!' (p. 527). Even Salieri eventually understands the extraordinary creativity in Mozart's
writing. While attending a performance of *The Marriage
of Figaro* Salieri marvels at his rival's achievement. He is
particularly awestruck by the closing ensemble from the
fourth act:

> The scene was night in a summer garden. Pinprick stars
> gleamed down on shaking summerhouses. Plotters
> glided behind pasteboard hedges. I saw a woman,
> dressed in her maid's clothes, hear her husband utter
> the first tender words he has offered her in years only
> because he thinks she is someone else. Could one catch
> a realer moment? And how except in a net of pure
> artifice?   (p. 534)

Shaffer's strong background in music lends cogency
and persuasiveness to these and other comments on music
in *Amadeus*. In interviews Shaffer explains that, along
with his novel views on the subject matter appropriate for
opera, Mozart's instrumental harmonies constituted a
challenge to the musical establishment of his day. His use

of chromatic passages especially unnerved eighteenth-century Austrians, as did his later works preparing the way for the Romantic age. In *Amadeus* Shaffer conveys these ideas in part through the Venticelli, who express the common Austrian response to Mozart's operas:

> v 1 [*complaining*]. It's too complicated!
> v 2 [*complaining*]. Too tiresome!
> v 1 All those weird harmonies!
> v 2 And never a good bang at the end of the songs so you know when to clap.   (p. 535)

The avant-garde in any epoch clearly disconcerts tradition-alists and must force its way to acceptance.[8]

In *Amadeus* Shaffer refines his stage methods to a new peak of effectiveness. Twice before (in *Royal Hunt* and *Equus*) and once since (in *Yonadab*) he has synchronised narration and action, but in *Amadeus* he exploits that technique to its fullest, thanks particularly to the exceptional fluidity with which the focus shifts between up-stage and down-stage acting areas. In the published playtext Shaffer includes a description of the set designed by John Bury. In Bury's award-winning design, a large rectangle of patterned wood down-stage centre led away from the audience to a façade of plastic panels which changed colour with the lighting. Most of the main action – especially the scenes set in Salieri's salon, Mozart's last quarters, various reception rooms and opera houses – took place within the rectangular space. At the back of the rectangle stood a grand and ornate proscenium accented by gilded cherubs and sustaining huge curtains of sky-blue. The curtains rose or parted to reveal a sizable enclosed space into which backdrops could be moved. Onto these, various images were projected: theatre boxes;

walls of mirrors and a huge fireplace representing the palace at Schönbrunn; and silhouettes of citizens as well as formal figures of nobility. Shaffer terms the up-stage space 'an immense rococo peepshow' as well as a Light Box.[9] Because *'the action is wholly continuous'* (p. 482), the author reminds his readers, a set permitting total fluidity is absolutely essential. There is no single focal image comparable to the dazzling sun icon of *Royal Hunt* or the astonishing horse figures of *Equus*, but the overall picture that the set descriptions and stage directions build is one of an opulent city driven by malicious rumours and public whim.

Visually and aurally, *Amadeus* emerges from Shaffer's script an ideal vehicle for his themes. Chief of these is his favourite theme of man's attempt to achieve reconciliation with a baffling and seemingly unjust god: but, when that universal topic is set within the specific context of Mozart's Vienna, abstract metaphysics become readily accessible. Personal rivalries, social antagonisms, political intrigues and artistic contrasts all fit into Shaffer's total framework. The important composer Antonio Salieri and the musical genius Wolfgang Amadeus Mozart become mere pawns in the grander debate that Shaffer dramatises: that between mortal man and his enigmatic deity. *Amadeus* so effectively and enjoyably deals with these matters that it seems likely to hold its place as Shaffer's *chef d'oeuvre*.

7
'Yonadab': Variations on a Favourite Theme

After the enormous international success of *Amadeus* six years earlier, interest in Peter Shaffer's next play, *Yonadab*, ran high. It received its premiere in 1985 at the National Theatre, London, where it played in repertory for a year and proved controversial yet moderately popular. Eager to match its success with Shaffer's previous play, the National assembled a strong team. The director (Peter Hall) and scene-designer (John Bury) were the same as for *Amadeus*. Alan Bates was cast in the challenging role of Yonadab, and respected performers such as Leigh Lawson, Anthony Head, Patrick Stewart and Wendy Morgan took other major parts. Yet critical reaction to the play was only lukewarm.[1]

Shaffer himself recognised deficiencies in *Yonadab*. Looking back later he acknowledged the London production 'was not complete . . . because in truth the play was not yet ripe'.[2] He insisted on reworking the script before

128

allowing a Broadway production. Revisions were quickly completed, but the New York staging was repeatedly postponed, owing to casting problems and the difficulty of fitting a new production into Peter Hall's busy work schedule. Eventually in 1989, before a US staging had materialised, Shaffer published the revised text. The result is that, while the only production so far has been the original, now supplanted version, the only available published text is of Shaffer's revision. The differences between the two versions shed valuable light on Shaffer's writing habits, as we shall see later in the chapter.

Yonadab draws on Peter Shaffer's favourite themes and techniques. In particular, the drama has affinities with *Amadeus*, furnishing a dark counterpart of the Salieri–Mozart schema. Thematically, the drama centres on Yonadab, a figure on the periphery of a court arena dominated by grander characters, King David and the princes Amnon and Absalom. As witness to the comings and goings of his royal superiors (Shaffer calls his protagonist the Watcher), Yonadab gradually wins the trust of the princes, his cousins, and comes to influence them. They become his means for probing the strengths – and limits – of Israel's god. In overall terms, Yonadab is one of Shaffer's familiar god-seekers, and the play a forum for speculation on metaphysical questions. Like Salieri in *Amadeus* and Dysart in *Equus*, Yonadab is both narrator and participant, and opens the play by addressing the audience directly as master of ceremonies. He speaks to us from his vantage point in the distant past, in this case a pre-Christian era, to offer his account of events in his day. As narrator he can freeze action on the stage to comment on it; as a player in the story he frequently turns aside from the audience to enter the illusion of the plot. Everything we see and hear is therefore mediated by him.

Biblical history and legend provided the initial inspiration for *Yonadab*. Set in King David's Jerusalem of around 1000 BC, the story derives mostly from 2 Samuel 13. The thirty-nine verses of the chapter recite details of sordid actions matching those of any contemporary fictional thriller. Sibling rivalry, incest, rape, fratricide, jealousy and betrayal are all involved. The Bible says little about Yonadab, or Jonadab as he is generally called in English translations. Yet the first few verses of the Samuel source (quoted here from the Authorised King James version of the Bible) hint darkly at his importance as a catalyst in the events related:

1   And it came to pass after this, that Absalom the Son of David had a fair sister, whose name was Tamar; and Amnon the son of David loved her.

2   And Amnon was so vexed, that he fell sick for his sister Tamar; for she was a virgin; and Amnon thought it hard for him to do anything to her.

3   But Amnon had a friend, whose name was Jonadab, the son of Shimeah David's brother: and Jonadab was a very subtil man.

Yonadab clearly is an influence on the subsequent events, even if he does not actually trigger them. It is on his urging, for instance, that Amnon tricks David into sending Tamar to him, thus giving him the opportunity to rape her. He also carries messages between the various parties, and is obviously privy to what is going on.

Shaffer acknowledges that, while he had known the story since childhood, it was a fictionalised account that stimulated him to centre a play on the shadowy figure of Yonadab. That account, a popular novel entitled *The Rape of Tamar* by the South African author Dan Jacob-

son, was his principal source.[3] Jacobson's book, drawing
on and expanding the biblical story, demonstrated its
dramatic potential. After meeting Jacobson and discuss-
ing the novel with him, Shaffer decided to treat the same
subject in a play.

A comparison of the novel and the play shows how
indebted Shaffer is to Jacobson's work. Like Jacobson he
adheres to the basic outline of the biblical story, which
needed no radical alteration to become a vehicle for
powerful drama. Briefly, the Bible tells that King David's
eldest son and heir presumptive, Amnon, falls into a
paralysing lust for his half-sister Tamar. Yonadab, a
cousin and confidant, suggests a ruse to get the unsuspect-
ing girl to come alone to Amnon's quarters. Unable to win
her consent to his sexual advances, Amnon loses patience
and rapes Tamar before flinging her naked into the streets
of Jerusalem. Tamar's reaction is surprising. She refuses
to accept humiliation passively by creeping back to her
father's palace. Instead, after ritually covering her head
with ashes, she wanders through the city streets in a
gesture of religious self-mortification. Tamar's brother
Absalom inquires about her intense distress and learns of
Amnon's treachery. He is furious with his half-brother for
the heinous act, but refrains from attacking him
openly – even when David, for reasons that the Bible
does not explain, refuses to take action on behalf of his
wronged daughter. Two years elapse while Absalom bides
his time. Eventually, he lures Amnon away from the
protection of David's palace and orders the rapist slain.
Fearing David's reaction, he then exiles himself from the
court.

Jacobson's novel ends at this point, with Amnon dead,
Absalom in exile and Yonadab disgraced. Shaffer takes
the tale further, to Absalom's death. Fleeing on a mule

from David's forces, Absalom accidentally catches his marvellously long, luxurious hair in the branches of a tree, and while suspended helplessly is discovered by soldiers and killed. The Bible (the source of this story) further adds that Solomon, another of David's numerous sons, subsequently inherits the throne of Israel. Shaffer's drama accommodates this development in an epilogue that looks forward to the break-up of David's once-glorious kingdom in chaos and internal strife.

Such are the biblical accounts of the sordid history of David's progeny. Yet many details remain ambiguous or are omitted altogether – especially the motivations of the protagonists. The imaginative writer is thus left a certain latitude in reconstructing these events. Yet, as in his previous period dramas, Peter Shaffer is primarily interested not in re-creating history but in exploring aspects of human behaviour, and, with this end in mind, he follows Jacobson in shifting the focus of the biblical story. At the centre stands not David, renowned King of Israel, but Yonadab, a familiar Shafferian seeker of metaphysical truths. Jacobson was the first to use the minor historical character as a lens for the story's action, allowing Yonadab (like Salieri in *Amadeus*) to speak to us today as a ghost from his own moment in history. Jacobson's Yonadab introduces himself as follows:

> it's always difficult to take the dead altogether seriously. What a dwarfish, slavish, disadvantaged race of spooks and less than spooks they are! . . . If, *per impossibile*, the dead could choose, each would doubtless choose the state other to the one he is in: the remembered would choose to be forgotten, the forgotten to be remembered . . . Now (and you may, if you wish, imagine me to be suitably dressed for my part

with my flesh and features arranged in a conventionally lifelike manner) allow me to introduce myself. My name is Yonadab. (*RT*, pp. 9–10)

The novel's narrator is similar to Shaffer's in the way he sets out the theme, but is more specific about the details: 'I am . . . embarrassed . . . by how commonplace, how drearily familiar you will find it all. Fraternal rivalries, incestuous desires, the struggles between a father and his sons, the greed for possessions and power . . .' (*RT*, p. 11). Shaffer's Yonadab also teases his audience, but is less matter-of-fact and more mysterious: 'This is a singularly unpleasant story . . . I alone know it all – and, let me assure you, I don't intend to spare yours [i.e. your ears] . . . This is a tale of total deceit. Every person in it is both deceiver and deceived. And I mean every single one. It is the true and secret story of the ruin of the House of David by me – his despised nephew' (*Y*, p. 87).

Shaffer's play, like Jacobson's novel, employs Yonadab as a mediator who reports his and others' machinations from behind the scenes. Yonadab parallels Iago in not performing the heinous acts himself but ingeniously instigating them. Though a subordinate in King David's court, he enjoys greater freedom of movement and greater privacy than do his celebrated princely cousins. He is free to think thoughts that they, in their exalted positions, dare not harbour, for fear of the numerous gossipy courtiers and hangers-on poised to intercept every unguarded remark. An opportunist, he seeks weaknesses and foibles in others and exploits them, tempting his victims by assuring them that their innermost desires *can* be realised. His method is simple but lethal. To convince Amnon to pursue his fantasies, he persuades him that they are no perverse sacrilege but a sacred right. Like the traditional

Satan archetype, Yonadab tempts by playing on the illicit desire already inherent in the victim. He woos Amnon's evil nature insidiously, declaring,

> I have read certain old parchments – absolutely forbidden, of course. The process is amazing. An image of his sister is sent into the Prince's head by the Gods. She doesn't even know it herself. She then torments him . . . He suffers horribly . . . But in the end, if he is worthy, he wins through! They couple together with a pleasure unimaginable to the rest of mankind – and achieve immortality!   (p. 100)

Yonadab's bait transcends Amnon's mere lust. The bogus prophecy also promises that Amnon will achieve godhead, transcending his mortal brothers and even David his royal father. It is a temptation too powerful to resist. At Yonadab's urging, Amnon determines to fulfil his desires in a dreadful act that ultimately will lead to his destruction.

Despite his unsavoury character, Yonadab becomes another of Shaffer's spellbinding protagonists, principally because of his cleverness and eloquence. *Yonadab* is Shaffer's ultimate Faustian parable. The tempter uses similar bait with Absalom, supposedly the righteous and unassailable one among David's sons. This time he varies the pitch, claiming that it is Amnon who insists that Absalom is God's chosen. Angrily, Yonadab with seeming reluctance repeats to Absalom a notion, attributed to Amnon: 'And he thinks you're Chosen! [*He laughs shrilly.*] *You – Prince of Peace!!* . . . He thinks bedding his sister can turn a Prince into a God . . . Yes, well now he thinks it's *you* . . . Not him – *you* who has been ordained, all the time! Quite a surprise, isn't it? He told me all the Signs for it this afternoon' (*Y*, p. 146). Tamar meanwhile has devised her own stratagems, and, when she joins to convince Absalom of their sacred match, the prince loses all resistance. The combination of a lovely bride (bodily satisfaction) and divine status (spiritual supremacy) proves too powerful a temptation for Absalom. He is willing to pursue any path to attain these twin goals. Tamar makes a single qualification: she and her brother cannot consummate their relationship until Absalom has taken revenge on Amnon for his unforgivable attack on her. Shaffer provides a surprise ending that reflects Tamar's new-found cunning as well as Absalom's eventual despair. For all pretenders in the play, divine aspirations bring only grief and death.

If *Yonadab* were only a string of salacious episodes it would not be worthy of serious attention. Yet it is based on far more than mere titilation. Of utmost importance is Yonadab's role as Shaffer's now-familiar seeker of divinity. The entire drama turns on the fact that Yonadab, the only character capable of metaphysical speculation, lacks the worldly power to test his ideas directly. In his search for answers, therefore, he manipulates his royal kin, first Amnon and later Absalom, to act on his behalf. He functions both as 'watcher' and as 'user' of those around him.

Like his Shafferian forebears, Yonadab doubts that any deity rules the universe. When rewriting the play, Shaffer moderated Yonadab's original acerbic observations, making him more sophisticated and guarded. Yonadab in the revised text says to the audience,

The Bible-readers amongst you no doubt assume that everyone in ancient Israel was a ramping, stamping Believer. Not true. That's propaganda. For a start,

there was me. Yonadab the Creep. That actually is
what you become when you bow to One God because
you're terrified of stones – but long in your heart for
another one altogether, who has no use of stones. To
put it bluntly, this religion was simply not good enough
for me.   (*Y*, p. 89)

Such cynicism matches that found in Shaffer's earlier
serious dramas, and it is especially crucial to this play.
Because of his profound scepticism Yonadab can act
wickedly without the least prick of conscience or self-
doubt. He ranks with such incarnations of evil as Satan
and Iago. The irreverence that he expresses allies him
with all those who rankle at the earthly limitations arbi-
tarily imposed by a universal order. The clearest statement of Yonadab's motivation appears when he announces his goal of destroying David's empire. Early in
the opening act Amnon, helpless in his lust for Tamar,
asks Yonadab for advice and solace. Sensing Amnon's
extreme vulnerability, Yonadab speaks his innermost
thoughts to the audience, revealing the basis of his
statagems:

There and then a demon sprang up in *me*! The one
which lives in the guts of all despised men waiting to be
summoned. A lust greater even than the one in him: to
bring things down. To make it happen – ruin! Ruin to
the great who sneer! To the House of David for whom I
didn't exist! Ruin even to the *God* of David!   (*Y*, p.98)

After first flattering the debauched prince, Yonadab
brilliantly rationalises Amnon's terrible obsession with
Tamar. He appeals to Amnon's pride and vanity as well as

his lust, insisting that only a select few qualify for such an unorthodox alliance. It is an option available 'Only to kings. And, of course, the sons of kings. No one else. *But for them it is actually ordained*' (*Y*, p. 99, emphasis added). Incest, according to Yonadab's bizarre interpretation, *can* be part of a holy ordained plan.

What Yonadab offers Amnon is nothing less than a promise of immortality – a promise that Amnon cannot resist. Yonadab admits mundane reasons for wanting Amnon to sate his lust with Tamar. He harbours a faint belief that men *can* become gods. In case not, however, he dares any universal deity to halt the sacrilegious plan he has set in motion. He sneers at God, 'Let him defend Himself! Prove that He exists, *finally*! Let *Him stop me* if He is there – Yaveh the Prohibitor!' (*Y*, p. 98). When the trick works and Tamar arrives at Amnon's quarters, Yonadab the voyeur asks only to watch the 'magical' coupling of the siblings. The rape is a stylised mime, unforgettable in performance. Amnon resorts to force when Tamar rebuffs his advances, first shedding his flimsy robe, then tearing off Tamar's clothing. The visual images which follow transform Yonadab – as they do the audience – into a participating witness of an eternal rite. Naked Amnon (his back to the spectators) stands poised over the prone girl before suddenly drawing the curtains surrounding his bed. Ever the voyeur, Yonadab from a hidden vantage point recites what he and we are witnessing, using descriptions steeped in religious imagery.

Here is the first of Peter Shaffer's dazzling *coups de théâtre* in this work. No clear view of the deed is possible because of the drawn curtains. The rape is depicted instead through flickering silhouettes projected against the side of the draped enclosure around the bedchamber. Shaffer's stage directions provide visual clues to the effect:

With increasing visibility the shadows of their bodies are thrown onto the curtain; immense black shapes enlarged and distorted by the lamps. During the following speech they make a series of abstract and strange shapes: a mysterious procession of glyphs. (*Y*, p. 127)

Yonadab reports,

All my life I remembered what I saw that night: the shadows – more terrible than bodies. The limbs thrown up on the curtains like the letters of some grotesque language formed long, long before writing. There on the fall of a Jerusalem drape I saw . . . the archaic alphabet of the Book of Lust.

Once the sexual attack is consummated – marked by a '*terrible, lingering, agonized moan*' (from Amnon, not Tamar, incidentally) – the mood of the ritualised enactment quickly alters. Amnon's coupling with his sister has failed abysmally to provide either physical pleasure or the ennobling religious experience that Yonadab promised. No gods emerge from the crucible of Amnon's lust. The violent act remains instead all too human, even bestial, hence Amnon's agonised moan of outrage following sexual climax. Far from a titillating sexual escapade, the rape in Shaffer's choreographed mime takes its place with the ritualised stabbing of horses' eyes in *Equus* and the violent garrotting of Atahuallpa in *The Royal Hunt of the Sun* as an unforgettable image of betrayed faith.

Yonadab's corrosive evil destroys the familial bonds of David's clan. Of more consequence is the challenge that Yonadab thereby directs at God, to prove that he exists. Just as Salieri toys with Mozart to stymie an unresponsive deity, Yonadab dares Israel's God to react to the impious deeds in King David's household. To close Act I, Yonadab shouts to the audience, 'Ruin! Ruin to the House of David! And I the ruiner! Yonadab the family joke – Lord over them all! Lord over Him too above – *Yaveh the Non-God*! Hadn't I proved that now up to the hilt? If He lived I'd have been dead beyond anyone's doubt' (*Y*, p. 131).

The parable has not been played out, however. The following events, Yonadab informs the audience, will lead to his own destruction too. His vulnerability grows from his flickering hope that mortal man *might* be able to attain godhead by behaving like a god – transcending man's rules simply by ignoring them. The mating of brother and sister is one such rule. Yet the ruiner of the House of David sees that Amnon's latest debauchery has failed miserably as a way of inducing epiphany. The itch to fuse humankind with godhead and to test God's existence overcomes Yonadab. In Act II, when he tempts Absalom with the same audacious and sacrilegious notions as had trapped Amnon, Yonadab revives his own hope for proof of an ultimate cosmic power. In the background Absalom and Tamar embrace and kiss, while down-stage a frenzied Yonadab describes for the audience the rush of emotions coursing through him:

In a trance I watched it happen. Those two enfold – mingling their beauties together. And for the first time in my life I knew the force of prayer. Yes! As they stood there, unmoving, I called to them without any sound his words, 'Let it be! Let it be! . . . Let there be an end to this world of blood-soaked worship – and to my own world too, which owns no worship! *Make me see it*! (*Y*, p. 160)

Yonadab parallels Peter Shaffer's previous serious dramas by providing a rich visual tapestry to satisfy the audience's desire for theatrical excitement, and by unfolding a life-and-death spiritual struggle through the twists and turns of the plot. The play differs, however, from his earlier works in the sensuality pervading it. His success in combining narration and action depends again on his ability to create an emblematic protagonist who manifests spiritual *Angst* and can register it provocatively for audiences. In this respect Yonadab rivals such earlier Shafferian *raisonneurs* as Pizarro, Dysart and Salieri. Like them, he probes man's metaphysical puzzles as well as human inadequacies. Shaffer remains one of the few contemporary playwrights who can make such puzzles the basis of effective drama.

To this point, we have surveyed the sources of *Yonadab*, how Shaffer used them, and his central themes in the play. Ultimate intentions for *Yonadab* emerge even more clearly through a comparison between the original and the revised versions. The revised play tells basically the same story, but is a good deal terser. The first act has only about two thirds the number of lines in its predecessor, and spends less time creating a specific ethos of David's court; as a result the thematic centrepoint is reached more quickly. Amnon's unsuccessful seduction of Tamar is abbreviated, and their dialogue before the rape contains no mention of Yonadab. Moreover, Amnon is given suggestive lines which point towards the mystical consummation that he expects: 'Tonight everything changes . . . Tomorrow it will all be different. Not to be even imagined' (*Y*, p. 121). There are fewer long asides making the play less like a novel in its treatment of the story and its meaning. This tightening of the script answers one criticism of the original London production, where the spraw-

ling, novelistic script tended to dilute the thrust of the
action. In significant ways, the reworked *Yonadab* defines
itself more deliberately as a stage play by diminishing the
fictional manner and incorporating more theatrical effects.

Though most of the major characters are little changed
in the revised version, there are two major exceptions:
Tamar and Yonadab. Tamar is depicted as more conniv-
ing and deliberate in her actions than before. Early in the
revised second act she argues vigorously for Absalom to
take revenge on Amnon, even enlisting the help of
Yonadab. In the original text, she would have nothing to
do with Yonadab at any time. Her eventual turning
against Absalom is now no last-minute decision, as it
originally seemed to be. Despite the pain she suffers in
abandoning her beloved Absalom, she displays adaman-
tine will and nerves of steel. Shaffer clarifies certain hazy
moments near the end of the play, especially those
involving Tamar. Vengeance has overcome all other con-
siderations, and she attributes her strength of purpose to a
cruel, insistent god:

> Do you think it cost me nothing? I wept every night for
> what I had to do. I cried up to the Lord on high, 'Don't
> make me! I can't do it!' But He wouldn't yield . . . In
> the end he helped me. He hardened my heart. He
> showed me there was no difference between the
> brothers. Not in the end. No difference: Bull or Beau-
> ty. (*Y*, p. 177)

After admitting that she did not really believe that she and
Absalom could attain godhead by killing Amnon and
living together, Tamar turns Absalom's men against him.
Forced to flee without armed forces or family support, he

141

is slain brutally, becoming another victim of Tamar's justice. Paradoxically, she claims that God gave her the strength to defeat Amnon, Absalom *and* Yonadab – even though Yonadab claims to have disproved the existence of God. This final new interplay of wills between Tamar and Yonadab is a welcome addition in Shaffer's revised script.

Shaffer delineates Tamar's role more sharply in the rewrite, and in the process makes her characterisation more convincing. In the original resolution of the play her shrill invectives disjointedly attack many evils, real and imagined.[4] Gloatingly, she lashes out indiscriminately at all men:

> This one's name was Amnon – firstborn of the King. Cursed be Amnon. Cursed be the King. Cursed be Absalom his brother, beloved of the King! . . . Go and tell it in Jerusalem, what has been done today by a woman. Tell them what a *slit* has done – made according to the will of God![5]

Shaffer adjusts the objective of this scene in the published version of the play. A confused feminist diatribe is replaced by a statement of personal, very human messianic goals, making it clear that Tamar's achievement is the antithesis of Yonadab's aspirations to godhead. Tamar now couches her bloody acts in the trappings of national and moral justice, not simple feminine vengeance:

> This is Amnon – son of the King. See what has been done to him today by Tamar, daughter of the King – handmaid of the God of Justice! See him – torn as he tore! Gashed as he gashed me! . . . Justice has returned to Israel. I have returned it.

Yonadab

She turns to the GUARDS.

Go tell it in Jerusalem wht has been done today in Ba'al
Hazoor. Go – I release you. Tell it to all you meet:
Tamar has made Israel whole again. She has sweetened
Israel in the nostrils of the Lord! . . . Tell the People
they are purified! (*Y*, pp. 178–9)

Yonadab's intention of taking revenge against a disappointing god is also more explicitly articulated in the
rewrite: for example, where he announces to David that
all the sons – except Amnon – are safe.[6] Just as Salieri
destroys Mozart to get at God, so Yonadab destroys
David to test Israel's god. Yonadab candidly states his
case to David:

Yes. It's true. I ruined your family. Yes . . I worked it
all. Your daughter ruined – your son speared like a
boar! And nothing stopped me! God did *nothing*! . . .
Why could you not have seen? Stopped me? Struck me
down? SHOWN ME – SHOWN ME HE IS?

(*Y*, p. 172)

Shaffer gains more than a better defined and motivated
Tamar in his reworking of her character. He also
introduces her as another direct adversary to Yonadab.
Tamar enters the revised plot as one more 'player' in the
complex of conflicts. The antagonism between Yonadab
and Amnon is clear enough in the first version, as are
Yonadab's disagreements with Absalom, David and, of
course, God. But the refashioned Tamar is the sole
character capable of outwitting Yonadab, and her dramatic relationships with Amnon and Absalom are more
clearly defined. As a result, the revised *Yonadab* offers

more dramatic conflicts than before, and the tauter script allows them to be better sustained.

Overall, the revisions to the text of *Yonadab* clarify without redrawing the play's thematic contours. The case is different in the area of theatrical presentation. When rewriting the play, Shaffer reconceptualised it to produce a more presentational work. The lead figures apart, the characters are now all-purpose, generalised figures without distinct personality traits. Nor is anything like a realistic set retained. The new stage directions describe the playing area as simply '*within a stage*'. Shaffer's original concept required much fuller decor, as may be seen from these stage directions for the first version:

> *Principally we are concerned with* KING DAVID'S *throne-room; with* AMNON's *living room and bedroom; and with the living room of* ABSALOM. *It is suggested that these rooms be indicated by different coloured awnings suspended over the areas concerned.*
>
> *This is very much a world of awnings: of rugs and cushions, lamps burning naked flames, and braziers. If possible there should be a large sky, on which we may see blazing noons, sunsets and starry nights over the city.*

Only the barest stage props are mentioned in the revised directions, whereas the original text gave explicit suggestions such as '*Most of the domestic objects boasting any noticeable style are copies of objects from grander cultures elsewhere: visual echoes of Babylon and Assyria*'. By making the setting less specific, Shaffer underscores the universality of his themes.

Shaffer's most ingenious and far-reaching alteration involves the characters. At least two dozen performers took part in the original version. In addition to the central characters, there were a plethora of non-speaking roles: *five* for David's 'other' sons (i.e. those other than Absalom and Amnon), *four* for Absalom's guards, *two* for Amnon's bondsmen, *two* for David's servants, and miscellaneous priests, porters, citizens of Jerusalem, and so on. The revised version employs a total of twelve actors to portray all the play's characters. Six lead parts are retained from the original text; Yonadab's father, Shimeah, is the only major character to be dropped altogether. Astonishingly, all the other roles – princes, servants, soldiers, citizens, priests – are assigned to just six actors called 'Helpers'. For these figures to serve in so many capacities, they must be essentially non-descript. Shaffer describes the six as garbed in white robes, *'their individual features . . . obliterated by white stocking masks'*. All visual individuality is thereby erased. Accordingly, these six provide no specific dialogue, only mimed action. They are described as *'all-purpose assistants: they make sounds, but they never speak dialogue. Their gestures are informed with a clearly read, graphic authority'* (*Y*, 83–4)

Through the use of non-individualised figures Shaffer clears the stage of potentially distracting characters inessential to the plot. Conversely, the focus on the central figures is more intense. The Helpers also impart a distinct ritualistic quality to the proceedings through their abstract appearance and mimed actions. This is a distinct advantage in certain scenes. Shaffer often ritualises climatic moments in his dramas when shocking – and possible unbelievable – actions take place. A striking example of ritual befitting a Greek *ekkyklema* occurs near the end of *Yonadab* when Tamar commands the six helpers (now guards) to bring in Amnon's body. When the bloody and naked corpse is carried in, lying across the guards' spears, Tamar launches into a bitter indictment.

Scenically, the moment becomes a negative ritual; instead of intoning paeans for the dead man, Tamar fills the air with curses.

The most riveting of all the ritualised moments in the second act is that of Amnon's slaughter (scene 12). Absalom has drawn his half-brother away from King David's protection by enticing him to the sheepshearer's feast at Ba'al Hazoor. Set in festive quarters, the scene features a huge woollen rug (centre-stage) emblazoned with the Star of David. The Helpers adopt different identities for this episode, and Absalom greets the unsuspicious Amnon:

> *He extends his hands to* AMNON *in peace. They embrace. The* HELPERS *clap their hands.* AMNON *takes the hands of each of the* HELPERS *(now brothers) in turn . . . Wild music breaks out. The* HELPERS *dance, shouting.* ABSALOM *rises and assists* AMNON *to rise. They dance together, as four* HELPERS *retire. At the height of their dancing – a sudden crash in the music. It breaks off.* TAMAR *stands there . . . She is flanked by Absalom's* GUARDS. *They are armed with their staves as usual but now the tips of them sport sharp metal points. The two* HELPERS, *still playing Princes, rush from the stage in panic . . . The* GUARDS *chase* AMNON *with their spears. He runs from them and, gargling with fear, finally burrows under the rug. Pitilessly the* GUARDS *drive their sharp weapons through it. A great stain of blood appears in the centre of the Star of David.* (*Y*, pp. 169–70)

Mime dominates the portrayal of the barbaric assassination. As in the rape episode – and, in earlier dramas, the scene where Salieri reads Mozart's scores, that where Alan Strang re-enacts his horseback ride, and the Mime of the Great Massacre from *Royal Hunt* – symbolic gesture supersedes verbal narrative. To escape the pending slaughter, the frenzied Amnon is shown ducking beneath the giant wool carpet, crawling his way towards its centre. Above him, the Helpers bang their wooden spears on the floor in synchronised rhythms, ritualistically re-creating the rhythms of sexual attack. The image of sexual assault is sustained when the guards thrust their spears into the wriggling man beneath the carpet, scarlet blood then oozing through. The result is a terrifying *coup de théâtre*.

The play's finest theatrical achievement belongs to its final scene. Shaffer combines a striking representation of the central theme with a visual tableau to make the moment unforgettable. Form and substance fuse in a horrific emblem whose full meaning is underscored by Yonadab's highly charged narrative. On learning of Tamar's betrayal of Absalom, Yonadab immediately understands its negative ramifications. Moving outside the action to resume his role as mediator, he analyses the outcome for each major protagonist in turn. Tamar, '*a Warrior-Priestess, self-intoxicated*', is seen stamping the floor and waving her spear triumphantly, then moving to the centre of the inner stage, where she sits behind Yonadab. She beats a small drum while chanting lines in which she gloats over her victory. The naked body of Amnon is meanwhile unceremoniously dumped downstage, at the edge of the outer stage. Yonadab responds to the scene, telling the audience that, though Tamar's revenge may have given meaning to her life, it has given none to his:

And she sat for life in her palace and sang to her savage God, the stink of vengeance the incense of her Faith . . . For life she sat, a Chosen Prophetess, and turned all her pain into meaning. And I sat banished on

147

my dreary estate, and knew *none*. No meaning. Ever.
One moment of hope – then dark for ever. . . . How I
despised her! And how I *envied* her!   (pp. 180–1)

While Yonadab narrates the conclusion to David's tragic
saga, Absalom's lifeless body is slowly lowered from high
above the stage, twisting and turning in mute commentary
on the violence characterising David's reign. At the same
time, David appears on the stage apron to lament Absalom's death. Yonadab reserves fierce scorn too for David:
'Always on me the curse of that man! [*He points to the
King.*] To watch for ever unmoved. To see the *gestures* of
faith in others, but no more' (*Y*, p. 181). Such scenes are
extraordinarily theatrical, even horrific, yet they are not
merely spectacle indulged for its own sake. Instead, they
effectively correlate action and thought.

With the help of his stunning stage effects Shaffer
documents mankind's condemnation to helpless uncer-
tainty over the existence and activity of a universal deity.
Yonadab's compulsion to fathom universal absolutes places him in the company of such earlier Shaffer protagonists as Pizarro, Dysart and Salieri. Yonadab's closing lines
marvellously encapsulate the typical stalemate concluding
each of Shaffer's God-seeking dramas: 'What choice, I ask
you, is this – between Belief and None, where each is
lethal?' (*Y*, p. 182).

8
'Lettice & Lovage': New Comedy for a New Age

Lettice & Lovage caught audiences off guard. After twenty years building an international career centred on serious drama, Peter Shaffer in 1987 suddenly returned to comedy. An entirely new generation was thus introduced to the less serious side of the award-winning playwright.

Older observers of his work, of course, remember the considerable comic talent that Shaffer displayed in the one-act comedies of two decades earlier. Though built on many of the same foundations, *Lettice & Lovage* constitutes a major advance. Here is a witty full-length work that engages its audience on many levels. The three-act format allows the dramatist latitude to create beguiling characters and to immerse them in social issues familiar to contemporary audiences. Moreover, the two leads are women. Never before had Shaffer centred his plot around female protagonists. *Lettice & Lovage* lays to rest allegations that he could not – or would not – write plays in which women took the lead. In addition, the several themes underlying *Lettice & Lovage* differ markedly from those in his previous dramas. Shaffer's preoccupation with divinity and mortality, typically framed in bleak metaphysical terms, plays no part here. Replacing austere universal topics are everyday situations involving ordinary persons. The overriding theme is the search of the protagonists for satisfying lives in a less than perfect society. Shaffer momentarily banishes God from the foreground. Remaining, however, is the dramatist's lifelong fascination with the duality of human nature: the desire for orderliness and security, on the one hand; and the will to trust one's intuition and risk the consequences, on the other.

Following a world premiére in Bath earlier in the month, *Lettice & Lovage* (known then as *Lettice and Lovage*)[1] opened at the Globe Theatre in London's West End on 27 October 1987. Shaffer was confident at the opening, and for good reason. He had an exceptional cast at his disposal for what is essentially a three-person piece. Maggie Smith played Lettice Douffet, a role written specially for her. The part of her antagonist, Charlotte (Lotte) Shoen, was performed by Margaret Tyzack, with Richard Pearson portraying Mr Bardolph, Lettice's frustrated solicitor. Directing was Michael Blakemore; Alan Tagg designed the set. Audiences responded immediately with strong enthusiasm, ensuring full houses and a successful run lasting nearly three years. Among the critics, Irving Wardle in *The Times* (28 October 1987) expressed strong support, declaring, 'It is an original and often hilarious treatment of an important and theatrically neglected subject; combining uproarious farce with savage indignation, and supplying ample opportunity for character development.' Charles Osborne wrote in the *Daily*

Telegraph (28 October 1987) that 'Peter Shaffer has written an original, highly entertaining and intelligent comedy', while Milton Shulman of the *Evening Standard* (28 October 1987) thought the play a 'pleasing comedy'. Not all reviewers were charmed. In the *Observer* (29 October 1987) Michael Ratcliffe claimed that 'whimsy' moved the plot 'into the land beyond belief', while Peter Kemp of the *Independent* (30 October 1987) judged the play to be 'made up of loosely looped together revue sketches'. Michael Billington's opening-night review in the *Guardian* (28 October 1987) called the play 'a whimsically enjoyable, if slightly overweight, conservationist comedy . . . in which the two halves of Peter Shaffer – the boulevard entertainer and the obsessive artist – conjoin'. During the first year of the run Maggie Smith and Margaret Tyzack shared London's top acting honours for their performances, helping to make the play a hit for several seasons.

Notwithstanding its great success, Peter Shaffer was not wholly satisfied with his script, though he permitted publication of the unrevised text. His revisions to the final moments of the third act, and other errant sections, produced a tightened version which replaced the original when the cast changed at the end of 1988, with Geraldine McEwen taking over from Smith. A New York production, with Smith and Tyzack repeating their London roles, was scheduled for early 1989, but Maggie Smith had a serious bicycle accident and the Broadway opening had to be delayed for over a year while she recuperated. The American première finally took place at the Ethel Barrymore Theatre, New York, on 25 March 1990. Paxton Whitehead took the role of Bardolph, and Michael Blakemore again directed. Smith and Tyzack elicited standing ovations from the start of the run; within two months both received Tony Awards, Smith for Best Leading Actress, Tyzack for Best Supporting Actress. Tony nominations also went to Shaffer for his play and to Blakemore for direction.

The American reviews, like the British, praised the acting of Maggie Smith and Margaret Tyzack, and approved of the script as an ideal vehicle for the actresses. Frank Rich of the *New York Times* (26 March 1990) deemed the play 'a slight if harmless confection that at first matches Miss Smith's bracing energy but by Act III must be bolstered by it'. Edith Oliver in the *New Yorker* (9 April 1990) called the comedy 'a source of continuous delight', and Jack Kroll of *Newsweek* (2 April 1990) suggested that it could be considered 'a pure draft of high-styled Wildean comedy'. Henry Popkin in *Theatre Week* (16 April 1990) announced that '*Lettice and Lovage* with its star, Maggie Smith, is surely the most effective laugh-machine that Broadway has seen in many years'.

The importance of the Lettice and Lotte characters, and the success of Maggie Smith and Margaret Tyzack in playing them, cannot be overstated. Nowhere in Shaffer's playwriting is the dominance of the Apollonian— Dionysian antithesis more pronounced than it is with these two unlikely protagonists. Lotte Schoen embodies the cool pragmatism and absolute adherence to 'rule' demanded of the Apollonian archetype; Lettice Douffet conversely trusts to instinct, surrounding herself with artifacts and 'facts' which give her personal and aesthetic pleasure. The need for effective casting of these two roles is thus quickly apparent. Neither character is portrayed as of great consequence in the world. Both are simply middle-aged spinsters who lead unexceptional lives in modern-day London. Shaffer addresses the question of living and working in today's technologically expanding world but without trying to provide wholesale solutions. Added to vocational perplexities are the women's personal concerns, particularly the problem of nurturing friendship and retaining individuality in a world that seems hostile to both. A related issue is society's destruction of people's sense of historical identity. As spokeswomen for the subversive erosion of England's heritage, both Lettice and Lotte decry the insensitive destruction of so many historically valuable (and beautiful) buildings in London, and their replacement with ugly monstrosities. In their eyes commercial materialism is excising England's past, to say nothing of its glory. Both women recognise the need for conservation, but not until the play's final act do their different approaches become reconciled. Amazingly, *Lettice & Lovage* draws attention to the collision of moral and aesthetic values in contemporary life while remaining a buoyant comedy.

Shaffer structures his play in three tightly focused acts. The first introduces Lettice Douffet in her baroque, eccentric extravagance. Much of Act II is devoted to creating the character of Charlotte Schoen. Discovering that they hold certain ideas in common, the two loners initiate a friendship. Act III reaches a comic climax when the alliance is ruptured by a misunderstanding; once all the facts are known, an upbeat reconciliation follows. The curtain scenes correlate with the central subject of each act: Act I concludes with a *coup de théâtre* centring on Lettice; Act II has a surprise ending featuring Lotte; and Act III brings the two heroines together in a final comic twist to the plot. Although each act evinces its own tonality and texture, the three acts form a harmonious whole.

The opening act consists of four episodes (in two scenes) delineating Lettice Douffet's brief and ill-fated career as a tourist guide. As a tour leader for the Preservation Trust (a slightly disguised version of the National Trust), Lettice is required to recite a prepared script for visitors touring a provincial estate. Described only as '*a lady in middle life*', Lettice is first seen standing before the grand staircase of Fustian House, a manor she later labels 'quite simply the dullest house in England!' (p. 22). The 'canned' history she must deliver suffocates all listeners with its dry factualness, and Lettice cannot rouse the motley group from dispirited boredom. In the second episode of scene 1, '*some days later*', we see her mechanically repeating the same spiel for another batch of uninterested listeners. About to lose the group's attention altogether, she resolves to awaken them to some sort of appreciation of Fustian House. Obviously well-versed in Elizabethan culture, she lightens the situation with esoteric facts extending back to the manor's heyday. Elizabethan eating habits suddenly take on significance when she interjects odd details concerning the cuisine of the time. Elizabethans, for instance, had a taste for hedgehogs, which they called 'urchins', and the foods of the time included such strange items as puffins and coney (rabbit). Lettice even uses the occasion to correct misconceptions concerning Candlemas.

Her burst of imagination leads to fanciful embroidering of the historical facts; it also wins her the group's interest and loyal admiration. At the same time, her fey charm is established, a combination of the garrulous and the endearing. Eventually Lettice crosses the line between colourful embellishment of facts and pure fancy, and rumours of her liberties with historical truth reach the ears of Miss Lotte Schoen, head of personnel at the Preservation Trust. In the final episode of the first scene, she comes unannounced to Fustian House and joins a tour.

Calling Lettice's bizarre tamperings with history 'intolerable', she then summons the errant guide to headquarters for inevitable dismissal.

The confrontation in Lotte's London office (Act I scene 2) expands on Lettice's background and upbringing. She defends her flights of fancy with the unforgettable credo 'Fantasy floods in where fact leaves a vacuum' (p. 25), and tells how her English mother, abandoned by a French husband, formed an all-female theatre troupe which crisscrossed the French countryside performing Shakespeare – in French, of course. Lettice's highly unorthodox upbringing has given her a unique outlook on language and English history: quoting her mother with another saying that has lent direction to her life she states, 'Language alone frees one . . . And History gives one place' (p. 24). As a philologist with a love for the culture and values of earlier epochs, Lettice understandably finds few occupations suited to her in contemporary society. This learned woman ironically becomes part of the hard-to-place unemployed of London.

The battle of wills between Lotte (the play's Apollonian authority figure) and Lettice (the Dionysian free spirit) centres on the sanctity of 'facts'. Citing her late mother, Lettice insists that one's prime duty is not to propagate dry data but to inspire the lives of others: 'Enlarge! Enliven! Enlighten!' (p. 22). The sceptical Lotte brusquely dismisses such premises: 'This is nonsense – all of it! They don't matter! . . . None of this matters – your mother – your childhood . . . I am not in the entertainment business – and nor are you. That is all. We are guarding a heritage. Not running a theatre' (pp. 26–7).

The first act closes with the battle lines clearly drawn. Lettice's idiosyncratic approach to modern life is in direct contrast to Lotte's pragmatic stance, with its concern for consequences. Despite a grand surprise exit at the close of Act ii, Fact wins out over Fantasy at the close of Act i when Lettice is formally dismissed.

The second act gives equal time to Lotte. Several weeks have passed since Lettice was fired, and meanwhile Lotte's conscience has nagged her for what she has done. So impressed was she by Lettice's spirited defence of her behaviour that she has tried to find her alternative employment. Act ii opens with Lotte arriving at Lettice's basement flat in Earl's Court with news of just such a job. The shabby apartment (the setting for both Acts ii and iii) clearly demonstrates Lettice's extraordinary individuality: mementos of her past – theatre posters, stage props and stage furniture – dominate the living room. Lettice is disinclined to speak with her 'executioner' when Lotte first arrives, but eventually recognises her good intentions. Hard feelings vanish as the women come to know each other personally. Soon they toast each other in celebration of the new job opportunity and their new-found comradeship. 'Quaff', an 'adaptation' of a powerful sixteenth-century brew (according to Lettice), serves as their toasting beverage. After numerous cups of quaff, Lotte loosens up enough to talk openly about herself. Unlike Lettice, whose casual upbringing introduced her to a world of make-believe, Lotte underwent a formal education.

Lotte's personality was shaped to a great extent by her father. For him, as a publisher of high-quality art books, contemporary Western civilisation no longer possessed the capacity to recognise beauty, and Lotte grew up imbued with his bleak outlook. She elaborates,

> He believed anybody born after 1940 has no real idea what visual civilization means – and never can have.

'There used to be such a thing as the Communal Eye,'
he'd say. 'It has been put out in our lifetime,
Lotte – yours and mine! The disgusting world we live in
now could simply not have been built when that eye
was open. The planners would have been torn limb
from limb – not given knighthoods!' (p. 51)

Lotte admits inheriting her father's 'disease' – that is, the
Communal Eyes which perceive the ugly reality of today:
'Yes, well I'm his daughter – and that's the whole
trouble . . . Because I have his eyes. It's all he left me,
and I don't want them. I wish I was blind, like everyone
else'. Life has disappointed her, and the resulting bitter-
ness explains her sour disposition. Significantly, her
cynical view of the desecration of beauty in the modern
world incorporates Peter Shaffer's own conviction of
London's fall from aesthetic grace. Lotte recalls the years
when the destruction, as witnessed by her and a suitor,
was gathering pace:

We used to walk through the city endlessly together,
watching it be destroyed. That was the true Age of
Destruction – the late fifties and sixties. You realize
the British destroyed London ultimately, not the Ger-
mans. There would be gangs of workmen all over the
place, bashing down our heritage. Whole terraces of
Georgian buildings crashing to the ground. I still see
those great balls of iron swinging against elegant
façades – street after street! All those fanlights shattering – enchanting little doorways – perfectly propor-
tioned windows, bash, bash, bash! – and no one stop-
ping it. (p. 52)

In the opening act, Lotte functions primarily as antagonist to the more arresting character of Lettice. In the second act she comes into her own: evidence of her sensitivity and taste, qualities which make a worthy counterpart to Lettice, provides the needed basis for the comedy's eventual climax and resolution. Through their initial conflict Shaffer emphasises the differences between his two leads: Lotte's life is shown to be built on scientific objectivity and certitude, Lettice's inclined towards the arts and humanistic learning of the past; Lotte's cold, analytical temperament contrasts with Lettice's emotional and impetuous eclecticism; Lotte weighs her words with care, while Lettice garnishes each thought with colourful wordplay. Opportunities for dramatic conflict thus abound in the women's clash of wills and values; it is the collision of their lifestyles that provides momentum to the plot. On this one key matter, though, Lotte and Lettice concur entirely: the need to preserve beauty in the crass commercial age. Shaffer transforms his unexceptional spinsters into agents of historical conscience. Both women, it turns out, deeply resent the contemporary world for ignoring, even desecrating, history. They are particularly unhappy with the aesthetic blindness of the age. They see the past glorious architectural face of London perverted by graceless new commercial and civic buildings. In their shared dismay at this process, they put aside other disagreements. *Lettice & Lovage* chronicles a fascinating tale of how two very different individuals come to unite against the encroaching coarseness of modern society.

By the end of Act II Shaffer has established common ground between the two ladies. A new element is developed to form the basis for the third act. We learn in passing that both Lotte and Lettice admire strong-willed figures from the past. They especially respect those individuals who brave social displeasure to stand up for their convictions. Daring persons such as these raise the human dignity of their own times and give their successors something to respect and value. Given the dismal state of the modern age as they perceive it, Lettice and Lotte conclude that something needs to be done, though as yet they are uncertain what:

> LOTTE.   This entire city is actually crammed with fanatics from all over the globe fighting medieval crusades on our ground. Isn't it time we became a little fanatic ourselves on its behalf? . . . people in the past would not have endured it. But, of course, they had spunk. There's no one left now with any spunk at all.
> LETTICE.   Just the Mere! . . . The Mere People! That's all who remain.   (p. 48)

Both women know they cannot turn back the clock. Nor does either feel capable of stemming the tide of mediocrity overtaking them. Lotte, the pragmatist, is the first to realise that some relief might be obtained through resort to Lettice's make-believe world. In a spectacular *coup de théâtre* concluding the second act, Lotte is swept into a symbolic enactment of a glorious deed in history. If life today furnishes no inspiration, one option is to appropriate it from the past through re-enacting a historical instance of noble human conduct. In this way one can always have a praiseworthy model to draw on. The two spinsters end up close friends, united by a belief that fantasy can counter a callous universe.[2]

Shaffer radically alters the texture of the play in Act III by shifting to the traditional comic elements of confusion

159

and misunderstanding. Lettice has inadvertently wounded Lotte during one of their historical enactments and is now charged with attempted murder. Lettice's solicitor (ironically named Bardolph) must fight to uncover the details of the accident, since Lettice does not want the embarrassing circumstances known.[3] As Bardolph reminds Lettice, 'Do you actually realize the situation you are in? You are charged by the police with a peculiarly unpleasant crime. You go to trial in less than five weeks, and you tell me nothing with which one can possible defend you' (p. 62). He finally convinces Lettice that she will be found guilty unless he can defend her. Shaffer's comedy thus takes on a darker tone.

Lettice reluctantly agrees to disclose the facts behind the accident. As a result the actions that unite Lettice and Lotte as friends – their historical charades – threaten both Lettice's liberty and Lotte's reputation at the Preservation Trust. With misgivings Lettice humorously explains the background:

It transpired that we both harboured an enthusiasm for the heroic figures of the Past. People of spunk, as she would say. Especially those whose distinction earned them death at the hands of the Mere . . . As we got to know each other better, we came more and more to sit upon the ground, as Shakespeare has it, and tell sad stories of the deaths of kings. Not just kings, of course: men and women of all conditions with regal hearts . . . In the end . . . we came not only tell the sad stories but to represent them . . . Recall in Show how a few monumental spirits turned History into Legend.

(p. 70)

The incredulous solicitor learns that Lotte's accident stemmed from one such enacted episode, the beheading of Charles I in 1649. Lettice's cat pounced on Lotte (playing the part of Charles) precisely when Lettice (as the executioner) was standing with the axe poised ready. With that the axe fell, cutting Lotte, and the neighbours, hearing the screams, called the police, who broke in and found Lotte lying in a pool of blood and Lettice standing over her with a bloodied axe. Lettice of course was arrested at once to await trial. What should have been horrifying instead sounds funny – ridiculous – as Lettice proceeds with her narrative. Bardolph becomes intrigued by the fantastical circumstances. And, when Lotte unexpectedly arrives on the scene, head bandaged, all three take roles in a re-enactment of the fateful charade. The moment is pure comedy as Lettice urges the staid Bardolph to play the drummer at King Charles' execution, to show what happened:

BARDOLPH.   Pam-tititi-pam! . . . Pam-tititi-pam! . . .
LETTICE.   More menace. It has to have more menace
. . . Remember these were the most dreadful
drums in England. They were announcing the end
of everything. (p. 86)

Lettice's defence is now clarified, but it also entails some crucial personal choices. Bardolph can defend Lettice successfully because he knows that the wounding was an accident. But all the circumstances will have to be explained if the defence is to succeed. Ridicule is sure to follow, he cautions, mimicking the judge's probable comments. 'I find it extraordinary that two ladies of mature years have nothing better to do than behave like a couple

of feeble-witted schoolgirls' (p. 89). Bardolph's advice
revives the issue initially dividing Lotte and Lettice to
speed the play toward its crisis. Make-believe Fantasy
again collides with legalistic Fact, repeating the play's
original clash of values. The question is, how far Lotte will
stand by her friend. Faced with public embarrassment and
loss of her job, she wavers. Apollonian by nature, she
favours orderliness in her life. The risk taken by entering
Lettice's world of whimsy is now bringing her shame. Her
hard-headed pragmatism resurfaces as she declares bitterly, 'I am a respected woman in a responsible and
enviable job. After the trial I'll never be able to enter my
office again . . . I will resign first thing in the morning' (p.
91). When Lettice protests, Lotte cuts her off short,
ironically adding, 'It's entirely my fault. If one embraces
the ridiculous – one ends up becoming ridiculous' (p. 86).
Lotte begins to leave, their friendship seemingly ruined.
Lettice is less afraid of the pending embarrassment and is
stunned by Lotte's statement that their alliance must end.

At this point in the plot Shaffer makes subtle but vital
revisions to the original text. By eliminating several lines
and redirecting others, he sharpens the focus and nips in
the bud an incipient sentimentalism that threatens to
slacken the pace. (In the earlier version Lettice is left
alone on stage, weeping, for many minutes before Lotte
returns for the denouement.) Lettice's confidence snaps.
Humiliated and shattered by Lotte's rejection, she admits
'*In a voice of sudden defeat*' (p. 86) her deepest phobias
and insecurities, and in the process speaks for many
ordinary persons today:

> You're wrong, when you say there's nothing ghostly
> about me. That's what *I am*. A ghost. Every day more.
> Every day there's something new I don't under-

stand. . . . It's like a mesh keeping me out – all the
new things, *your* things. Computers. Screens. Bleeps
and buttons. Processors. Every day more . . . Bank
cards – phone cards – software – discs! JVC. PLC.
ABC. DEF . . . The whole place – the whole world I
understand isn't there . . . You're right. That's the
precise word for me – ridiculous. Ridiculous and useless. (p. 93)

Lettice's heartfelt admissions are heard silently by Lotte,
who sees more clearly how essential their friendship has
become for her. Lotte is also disconcerted by the apparent
destruction of the 'spunk' that she had admired in her
friend. Lettice's confession changes Lotte's mind about
leaving; determinedly she re-enters the flat to redeem
their association. In Shaffer's revised resolution, the moti-
vational logic is straightened out so that Lotte, not
Lettice, insists they should face the crisis together. It is
also Lotte who now first proposes a plausible solution by
refocusing their attention on the conservationist ideology
they share. Lotte proposes that they set up a tour called
the   END – The   Eyesore   Negation   Detachment – focusing on the fifty ugliest new buildings in
London. Lettice would guide and narrate the tour; Lotte
would provide specific data concerning the owners and
architects of the eyesores. Lettice instantly sees the possibilities and responds delightedly to what she calls 'the
single most theatrical idea I ever heard' (p. 96). With a
battle plan to combat the architectural boors menacing
London's landscape, the spinsters are wholly reanimated
by the comedy's end.

Peter Shaffer matches current audience interest well
with *Lettice & Lovage*. His themes of conservation and a
regard for the past represent concerns shared by many in

Western countries. Prince Charles, for example, has crusaded energetically against the architectural blotches dominating the skylines of more and more cities in Britain and in the United States.[4] Never before in his stage works has Shaffer focused with a conservationist's ardour on the need to preserve the past. But the subject has evidently been brewing in his mind for a long time. His film script for *Equus* indirectly criticises urban decay and governmental insensitivity to the preservation of historical sites. *Shrivings* alludes to the great need for shared historical and cultural values. Before *Lettice & Lovage* Shaffer's fullest treatment of the heritage theme was the radio drama *The Prodigal Father*, but there it lacks the strong central focus on the need for conservation.

Lettice & Lovage is in one way a successful throwback to the brilliant social comedy of Oscar Wilde and Bernard Shaw. Like them Shaffer possesses a gift for creating unique memorable characters and dazzling witty dialogue. No profound story lends ballast to the play, which is based on typical comic situation that permits the zany characters to show off their eccentricities, but the razor-sharp dialogue that, in the absence of strongly visual expressions of confrontation, is essential to keep the story moving is there in abundance. In *Lettice & Lovage* Shaffer proves that he can write an extraordinarily funny full-length comedy, as well as effective serious plays and comic one-acters.

Lettice & Lovage impressively juxtaposes, then conjoins, the Apollonian and Dionysian impulses within us. Shaffer's earlier Apollonian characters (Pizarro, Dysart, Salieri, Yonadab) are left unfulfilled because they cannot sufficiently reconcile themselves to their Dionysian antagonists (Atahuallpa, Alan Strang, Mozart, Amnon).[5] Even in previous comedies, the dénouements have a bittersweet quality and the resolutions are consequently incomplete. But we require both order and creativity in our lives if we are to be whole personalities, and that necessitates a compromise between the two sides of our natures. *Lettice & Lovage* forges a credible alliance between characters dedicated to divergent Apollonian and Dionysian values. Whether the conclusion of *Lettice & Lovage* signals a new direction in Peter Shaffer's work cannot yet be known. What is evident is that he can move beyond the *Sturm und Drang* of his previous writing to produce scintillating comedy which delights the spirit.

9
Speculations — Present and Future

This concluding chapter in truth concludes nothing. Peter Shaffer is still actively writing, and at the end of 1990 has several intriguing projects nearing completion. Artistically, his powers are at a peak, as the crystalline ideas and tight dialogue of *Lettice & Lovage* bear witness. His popularity in theatre circles is in general remarkably high. Few playwrights today can claim to have won as many prestigious awards as he has, including Tonys and an Oscar. Moreover, he is not only a serious dramatist, but has enjoyed considerable commercial success, so that he is welcomed in the West End and Broadway as promptly as at the subsidised National Theatre, where many of his foremost hits were premiéred. In fact, this success has spawned resentment among some critics, who seem to equate popularity with artistic poverty.

One paradox arising from Shaffer's financial success concerns his new power and the responsibilities accompanying fame. On the one hand, thanks to his celebrity, he

166

can insist on top directors and actors for his works. Even with plays that have not done as well as expected (i.e. *The Battle of Shrivings* and *Yonadab*) he has enjoyed the benefit of front-rank talent. And, because of his reputation and the all-out success of *Lettice & Lovage* in London, the playwright was able to delay that play's Broadway opening for a year, until Maggie Smith had recovered from a physical injury. (Maggie Smith and Margaret Tyzack went on in 1990, when the play eventually opened, to win Tonys for their performances.) On the other hand, Shaffer is careful with Broadway productions of his plays: because of the extraordinary costs involved, he refuses to allow his dramas to be produced in New York before appropriate artists are available. One consequence of this is that Broadway will not see *Yonadab* until artistic conditions are 'right', even though he would be guaranteed personal financial reward whatever the box-office receipts.

From today's vantage point, it is possible to recognise a number of basic features of Peter Shaffer's dramatic writing. His playwriting has evolved in a variable but discernible pattern. Naturalism pervades *Five Finger Exercise*, his first stage play, which proved at the outset his mastery of the well-made play format. The fact that he already had written a draft of *Royal Hunt*, however, suggests that he was eager to reach beyond the realistic idiom into epic and grand spectacle. Some may argue that, despite its obvious power and fascination, *Royal Hunt* suffers from problems of organisation and form, as well as from stretches of over-ripe language. Even so, the play was a watershed in the fledgling dramatist's career, for it opened to him the magic of theatrical illusion built on visual symbols and rich expressive features in the traditionn of 'total theatre'. Thus, after just two full-length plays

Shaffer had experimented with two widely contrasting sets of theatre techniques. All his subsequent plays would fall somewhere between the poles marked by those antithetical approaches.

At the same time as he was exploring different dramatic concepts, Shaffer was clarifying the principal themes which would appear in all his subsequent works. The contest between Clive and Walter in *Five Finger Exercise* suggested an Apollonian–Dionysian design, although in *Royal Hunt* and in *The Battle of Shrivings* the edges of his characterisations became smeared. Not until *Equus*, *Amadeus* and *Lettice & Lovage* did Shaffer present wholly clear portrayals of the psychic contest within us – a war in which the desire for order is pitted against an irrational, sometimes erratic intuition fuelled by personal desires. The muted response to both *The Battle of Shrivings* and *Yonadab* may well reflect those dramas' failure to convey the intended Apollonian–Dionysian structure convincingly.[1]

For an understanding of how the psychic duality in the Apollonian and Dionysian conflict functions, one should look at Shaffer's three most popular works – *Equus, Amadeus* and *Lettice & Lovage*. In each, the psychological and metaphysical differences between the chief antagonists are crystal clear, as our earlier discussion has shown. Also evident, when we look closely at these characters, is a still more universal pattern: each play starts with a 'proto-character' (not yet realised) brought into contact with an idea (which gradually flowers into theme). Like real human beings, Shaffer's proto-characters embody multiple 'selves' each of which perceives and interprets phenomena in its own way; the interplay of these 'selves' produces the composite outlook of what in real life is the mature self. But, because no single dramatic character can project all the insights gathered by the separate 'selves' Shaffer uses a literary prism to separate the discrete viewpoints and apportion them to different dramatic characters. Thus, the Apollonian and the Dionysian perspectives are the two most significant but not the only viewpoints that Shaffer seeks to express. To convey these key polarities, he creates two distinct characters in the plot, to reflect what is for him the major schism in our natures. A fuller perception of society is to some degree refracted by the range of characters in the work, whose different insights help formulate the world of the play.

With *Equus* Shaffer attained for the first time an almost ideal balance of dazzling form and probing theme. Like *Royal Hunt*, *Equus* has an episodic structure, but it is pared down to keep the plot and characters clearly in focus. John Dexter's guiding hand is evident in the visual dimensions of the script (Dexter once called himself a play's 'visualiser'), suggesting that the director also learned from his experience of working with Shaffer. Impressive as the original staging for *Royal Hunt* was, it lacked the uncluttered clarity that marked the production of *Equus*. *Equus* was and remains a remarkably impressive work as social commentary and as theatre.

Amadeus signals the apex of Shaffer's career so far, however. This is not to say that it is a 'better' play than *Equus*, but its subject extends beyond the domestic perimeters of *Equus* into the metaphysical realm that Shaffer had hoped to penetrate in earlier works. Mozart certainly qualifies as an enticing subject for a play, and Shaffer's unflagging interest in the conundrums of detective stories was put to good use in *Amadeus*. As noted earlier, *Amadeus* achieves a happy balance of acute suspense, stimulating philosophical speculation and brilliant theatrical fireworks. Shaffer has almost everything 'right' in this play which also offers a fascinating duel between two strong protagonists. Musicologists remain incensed at what they consider a sacrilegious protrayal of Mozart, but their ire is sadly misguided. A dispassionate consideration of the play at once reveals the author's intense affection for the musical genius who, after all, is the sympathetic victim of the tale. Shaffer never pretends that *Amadeus* is meant as an historical account of Mozart's life; like all effective playwrights – Shakespeare foremost – Shaffer uses historical figures for 'dramatic' purposes. Moreover, it should be evident that Antionio Salieri, not Mozart, has more cause to cry 'foul'. But, even with Salieri, Shaffer claims dramatic justification for his alterations to history. Perhaps the heat generated is a testimonial to Shaffer's effectiveness in making his protagonists so believable as characters.

Commenting further on *Yonadab* is unproductive for the time being. Shaffer is determined to produce the revised version in New York when the right performers and director are available. For now we can say that the theme of the original *Yonadab* was not sufficient to support the richly stylised production staged in London. But the resounding success of *Lettice & Lovage*, both in London and in America, is interesting for several reasons. First, the play marks Shaffer's return to comedy after a gap of twenty-five years. Secondly, it also marks a return to dramatic realism (the mode of all his comedies), with no mediators and no episodic schema. Thirdly, it is set in the present day, unlike its immediate predecessors *Amadeus* and *Yonadab*.

But the most striking thing about *Lettice & Lovage* is that the central characters are women. The Apollonian and Dionysian duality certainly figures prominently here, as it does in Shaffer's other major dramas; yet the playwright does not simply switch the gender of his protagonists, as a few commentators suggest. Lettice Douffet and Lotte Schoen are fully developed as *female* characters, and are 'believable' as such.

As though to reaffirm his ability to write women's roles, Shaffer has centred his most recent play – a seventy-minute radio play called *Whom Do I Have the Honour of Addressing?* – on a plight of a woman. Moreover, he has further plans for this play. Originally broadcast by the BBC in 1989 as a one-person comic monologue, this piece may next be seen as well as heard in an expanded television or stage adaptation.[2] The play is set in the flat of Mrs Angela Sutcliffe, co-proprietress of Swift Scripts Limited, a London typing firm specialising in movie and television scripts. In its present form, the one-character play is simply a long but comical suicide statement, clumsily read into a tape-recorder by the heroine. Angela, a middle-aged Englishwoman, is another of Shaffer's eccentric women characters who, like Lettice Douffet, insists on her independence and individuality. She has determined that the world will know precisely why she intends to take her own life.

Suicide, of course, is no laughing matter. But Shaffer has written a comedy here, and the play's opening lines establish a non-threatening tone immediately. Angela garrulously and comically addresses the unknown listener of the tape she is recording:

Hallo, Posterity. This is Eleven Dawlish Road, Clapham, London. Thursday evening, March the whatever. You are about to hear the only statement ever made by me, Mrs Angela Sutcliffe, concerning her life. Emendation: her life and death . . . No doubt the latter will be of considerably more interest, especially to those people who make their living from scandals. Journalists and so forth.[3]

Angela's life story involves a young Hollywood screen idol, Tom Prance, who convinces her to move to Los Angeles and head the office of a foundation that he has established for the needy. Angela quickly discovers certain truths – some comical, some otherwise – and returns to London, feeling betrayed. Her suicide tape recounts the events in America that led her to consider doing away with herself. By the end of the taped statement, which is filled with humorous digressions and friendly chit-chat, the audience knows for certain that Angela will not take her life after all. The tape serves as a comic release or catharsis, permitting her to carry on in a flawed world.

A second playscript, in and out of Shaffer's typewriter for over ten years, is nearly finished.[4] Shaffer still alludes to this piece as his Greek play because it is set in Greece. He remains tight-lipped about the details, stating only that it is a mystery drama concerning a successful playwright who dies (perhaps by murder) before his last drama is completed. The dead man's widow continues to find different last scenes for the play among her husband's effects and at the publisher's insistence must somehow determine which version is the correct one. At first it might seem that this is a detective drama reminiscent of Shaffer's earliest writing, where murder mysteries and the investigations dominate the action. But Shaffer's sketchy description of the techniques used with this unnamed play suggests a fresh and inventive format. He hints that three different actions will run on stage simultaneously: one concerning the playwright and his wife; a second showing enacted scenes from the playwright's unfinished script; and a third involving the wife and her son after the father's death. Audiences must wait to learn just how much of Shaffer's description will fit the finished work. What does seem evident, however, is the continuing appeal of suspense stories for Shaffer. His taste for verbal puzzles, reflected even in the titles for many of his plays, continues, as does his fascination with mysteries and investigations.

So, what ultimately can be concluded about Peter Shaffer at this point in his career? With regard to dramatic format, he seems wholly comfortable with realism, if the popular triumph of his recent *Lettice & Lovage* is any indication. Nor is that surprising, given that he grew up in the 1930s and 1940s. His latest stage triumph also shows that he has developed an increased interest in certain popular political and cultural causes. Shaffer maintains homes in both London and New York, dividing his time between the two. He is thus in touch with the theatrical currents of both Britain and the United States. He is alarmed by what he perceives as the West's self-destruction of its heritage and culture, the theme so prominent in *Lettice & Lovage*. He especially fears that belief in the value of intellectual and artistic endeavour is falling prey to the wrong-headed-notion that excellence equates to political elitism. For someone so articulate with the written word, such an idea is blasphemous and foolish. Egged on by issues such as these that touch on the fate of art, Shaffer may temporarily put aside his metaphysical quests to pursue contemporary activist themes. As Sheridan Morley explains, 'Shaffer has always been able, even in the heart of the commercial theatrical jungle, to engage an audience in adult and literate debate about the way we live now.'[5]

Yet a deeper current runs beneath the surface of Shaffer's writing which hints at a more profound, personal agenda for the dramatist. Throughout his career he has admitted when pressed that he continues to search for proof that God either exists or does not exist. Unless he has found his answer, it seems unlikely that he will be able to ignore basic metaphysical questions in his future work. He has dealt with grand universal themes in the past, making it doubtful that he can be happy working with mundane domestic matters indefinitely. Furthermore, the inner excitement that surfaces when Shaffer talks about his fresh visualisation of *Yonadab* reflects his continued attraction to innovative stage techniques that transcend modern realism. Nor do any of his recent comments suggest that he has satisfied his impulse to explore different theatrical modes. *Royal Hunt*, *Equus* and *Amadeus* are three of the boldest theatrical enterprises to have attracted both popular and critical acclaim. Nothing now suggests that Shaffer thinks he has said his final word on theatre tactics. Our best prognosis is that he will continue to range among traditional and experimental theatre forms for the rest of his career.

One factor that may cause Shaffer difficulty in his continued quest for theatrical freshness is the dearth of gifted directors able to translate his rich language into a brilliantly visualised staging. A case in point is *Yonadab*. Sir Peter Hall directed the original London production at the National Theatre in 1985. Shaffer, as he always does, immediately began rewrites. A completely refashioned version was completed within months, in ample time for a Broadway staging in 1986 or 1987. When casting difficulties delayed rehearsals in New York, Hall's availability to direct vanished in the swirl of other projects. Without Hall's direction – given the unique style of the revised script – Shaffer had no alternative but to postpone the American production of *Yonadab*. And, even as late as 1990, neither Hall nor a comparably talented director has signed on for Shaffer's provocative drama.

More devastating from Shaffer's personal perspective was the death in 1990 of John Dexter. Though he had not worked with Shaffer for a dozen or so years, Dexter none the less remained one of the most brilliant and successful directors of Shaffer's dramas. With Dexter's death, Shaffer expressed momentary despair, claiming him to be one of the very few directors who could give his scripts worthwhile theatrical treatment.[6] The danger is that a dearth of suitable directors will tempt Peter Shaffer and other boldly imaginative playwrights to stop producing adventurous scripts and rely instead on conventional plays with conventional direction.

Barring this, however, the chances are good that Peter Shaffer will carry on producing compelling dramas in a variety of styles, both traditional and daring.

1. Peter Shaffer and his Early Career: The Novels and Broadcast Plays

1. Larry D. Bouchard, *Tragic Method and Tragic Theology: Evil in Contemporary Drama and Religious Thought* (University Park, Pa, and London: Pennsylvania State University Press, 1989) p. 178.

2. Simon Trussler, General Editor's Introduction to *File on Shaffer*, compiled by Virginia Cooke and Malcolm Page (London and New York: Methuen, 1987) p. 6. There are few large-scale studies of the making of Peter Shaffer's art. Among the better commentaries (aside from Cooke and Page's notes) are Dennis A. Klein, *Peter Shaffer* (Boston, Mass.: Twayne, 1979); Gene A. Plunka, *Peter Shaffer: Roles, Rites, and Rituals in the Theatre* (Cranbury, NJ: Fairleigh Dickinson University Press, 1988); and John Russell Taylor, *Peter Shaffer*, Writers and their Work no. 244 (Harlow, Essex: Longman, 1974).

3. See Michael Hinden, 'When Playwrights Talk to God: Peter Shaffer and the Legacy of O'Neill', *Comparative Drama*, XVI, no. 1 (Spring 1982) 49–63.

4. I am very grateful to Peter Shaffer for my interviews with him over the past ten years, and have also benefited from the following interviews published by others: Tom Buckley, ' "Write Me", Said the Play to Peter Shaffer', *New York Times Magazine*, 13 Apr 1975, p. 20ff; Brian Connell, 'The Two Sides of Theatre's Agorized Perfectionist', *The Times*, 28 Apr 1980, 7; Roland Gelatt, 'Mostly *Amadeus*', *Horizon*, Sept 1984, pp. 49–52; Mel Gussow, 'Shaffer Details a Mind's Journey in *Equus*', *New York Times*, 24 Oct 1974, p. 50; and the interviews reported in Plunka, *Peter Shaffer*.

5. *The Woman in the Wardrobe. A Light-hearted Detective Story* was first published in London in 1951 by Evans Brothers; no American edition has been issued. Although 'Peter Antony' is listed as author, Shaffer wrote this novel alone. *How Doth the Little Crocodile? A Mr Verity Detective Story* (London: Evans Brothers, 1952) was also published under the name of 'Peter Antony', but this time Peter and Anthony Shaffer were joint authors. The edition published in the United States in 1957 dropped the pseudonym and appeared under the authors' joint names. *Withered Murder* (London: Macmillan, 1955) appeared in an American edition in 1956. Both editions give 'A. and P. Shaffer' as authors.

6. The detective here is named 'Fathom', and the Shaffers again indulge in wordplay, since the name indicates a probing quality. It is puzzling that the name Verity was dropped, as Fathom is essentially the same character, fat and with a passion for *objets d'arts*.

7. Anthony Shaffer's most successful work for the stage is the detective thriller *Sleuth* (1970), which won a Tony

Award and ran for over 1200 performances on Broadway. His drama *Murderer* (1975) proved less popular, but his writing – including some film scripts – has remained centred on mystery thrillers. He says he also continues to write stage dramas.

8. Aside from *The Public Eye*, Shaffer's comedies do not appear to follow the same structure. Only *White Liars* vaguely approximates the pattern of mystery fiction, because of its ironic, conflicting versions of the true facts involved.

9. See Martin Esslin, 'Drama and the Media in Britain', *Modern Drama*, XXVIII, no. 1 (Mar 1985) 99; and Ian Rodger, *Radio Drama* (London: Macmillan, 1982).

10. From Connell's interview in *The Times*, 28 Apr 1980, p. 7.

11. Shaffer writes, '[In] The Salt Land I attempted to construct a tragedy along loosely classical lines, not for the sake of experiment . . . but because the subject of Israel and immigration is truly heroic, and deserves classical treatment' – 'Labels Aren't for Playwrights', *Theatre Arts*, XLIV (Feb 1960) 20–1.

12. Additional details concerning *The Merry Roosters Panto* are available in Plunka, *Peter Shaffer*, p. 69; and in Cooke and Page, *File on Shaffer*, pp. 21–2.

13. *Whom Do I have the Honour of Addressing?* is scheduled for publication by André Deutsch, London. In the meantime, I am indebted to Peter Shaffer for providing a manuscript of the play.

2. Launching a Theatre Career: 'Five Finger Exercise'

1. Peter Shaffer, Preface to *The Collected Plays* (New York: Harmony Books, 1982) p. viii. All quotations from

the Preface and *Five Finger Exercise* are taken from this edition. Page references are given in parentheses following quotations.

2. Bouchard, *Tragic Method and Tragic Theology*, p. 179.

3. Quoted in Plunka, *Peter Shaffer*, p. 73. Other details concerning Shaffer's upbringing are available in Klein, *Peter Shaffer*.

4. Movie-makers saw possibilities in Shaffer's psychological drama, and a film adaptation was made in 1962 featuring Rosalind Russell, Maximilian Schell and Jack Hawkins. For convenience of filming, the scene was transferred from an English cottage in Suffolk to a striking modern home on the Pacific coastline near Carmel, California. Also, a more hopeful ending was added, showing Walter receiving mental care after being saved from suicide.

3. Four One-Act Comedies and 'Shrivings'

1. Shaffer's Preface to *The Collected Plays* (especially pp. ix–xiii) provides first-hand details regarding the writing of the one-acters. All quotations from the Preface, the one-act comedies and *Shrivings* are taken from this edition. Page references are given in parentheses after quotations.

2. Interestingly, *The Times* (11 May 1962) initially carried lukewarm reviews of both one-acters. Later, when reviewing different stagings with different casts, the anonymous *Times* critic admitted that the changes had substantially improved *The Private Ear* (10 Sep 1963).

3. In his review for the *Nation* (9 Nov 1963) of the first one-acters, Harold Clurman notes excessive cleverness,

yet also acknowledges Shaffer's growing dramatic versatility.

4. Gene Plunka comments on Shaffer's use of music in *Peter Shaffer*. Ironically, the 1988 Tony Award for best play was given to another small-scale play, *M. Butterfly* by David Henry Hwang, which also is built around Puccini's opera.

5. A movie of *The Public Eye* was made in 1972, directed by British director Carol Reed.

6. In the Preface to the *Collected Plays*, Shaffer admits that the title *Black Comedy* seems to mislead American audiences, for whom 'black' elicits distinct racial and political associations. He writes, 'Some people thought that I had written a propaganda play about blacks. I suppose I should have called it *Light Comedy*, an equally good title, and one far more appropriate for New York' (p. xiii). He has also mentioned 'Dark Comedy' as a possible alternative title.

4. Widening the Creative Lens: 'The Royal Hunt of the Sun'

1. All quotations from the Preface and *The Royal Hunt of the Sun* are taken from *The Collected Plays*; the page references following quotations relate to this edition.

2. One problem noted by some American reviewers was Shaffer's tendency to overwrite – a criticism that dogs his later plays as well.

3. Shaffer's long battle against literalism has erupted most openly when films have been made of his plays. A British film of *Royal Hunt* was made in 1969, featuring Christopher Plummer as Atahuallpa and Robert Shaw as Pizarro. The general opinion is that it was an expensive

flop. During my interviews with Shaffer in 1980, he denied any connection with the film, adding, 'It taught me a lesson in a way; I mean, I shall never not do my own films again. It was terrible.' But, even when he has been directly involved in plans to film his plays, difficulties have not always been totally avoided.

4. During those same interviews in 1980, Shaffer said he was baffled that some critics decried the 'theatricality' of his plays. Insisting that theatrical devices specifically belong in the theatre, he pointed out that critics never attack painters for being 'painterly' in their work.

5. Interestingly, old rumours that much of Atahuallpa's ransom had never been shipped to Spain but had been hidden away in South American mountain caves resurfaced in the late 1980s. Expeditions to locate the gold have been mounted. The 'hunt' continues.

6. Observers of the play frequently point out resemblances between it and Antonin Artaud's projected but never-completed *La Conquête de Mexique*. Artaud's appears to have been a far more ambitious treatment of the same historical source.

7. There are traces here of a modern 'primitive' or 'noble savage', reappearing also in *Equus* and *Amadeus*.

8. John Russell Taylor, 'Shaffer and the Incas', *Plays and Players*, Apr 1964, pp. 12–13. A helpful account of the play's workings is found in James Stacy's 'The Sun and the Horse: Peter Shaffer's Search for Worship', *Educational Theatre Journal*, 28 (Oct 1976) 325–35.

9. Taylor, 'Shaffer and the Incas'.

10. Robert Brustein exemplifies the divided response of some critics. Bluntly calling the debate in *Royal Hunt* 'Shaffer's long-winded pseudo-Lawrentian mulings', he none the less applauded the play's theatricality as a 'vibrant visual display' which 'drew on all the possibilities

of the stage and all the magnificence of an exotic Peruvian culture' – *The Third Theatre* (New York: Alfred A. Knopf, 1969) pp. 112–13.

11. Gene Plunka mentions the round-table session on Artaud in his book (*Peter Shaffer*, p. 44) and provides comments regarding possible connections between *Royal Hunt* and Artaud's work on the Spanish conquistadors in Mexico. See Plunka, *Peter Shaffer*; and Klein, *Peter Shaffer*.

12. Review of *Royal Hunt* by B. A. Young in the *Financial Times*, 8 July 1964.

5. 'Equus' and the Mature Shaffer

1. See details in C. J. Gianakaris, 'Drama into Film: The Shaffer Situation', *Modern Drama*, XXVIII (Mar 1985) 87–97.

2. The initial critical response was not entirely unanimous, however. Ian Christie in the London *Daily Express* (27 July 1973) fulminated against *Equus* as pretentious and philosophical claptrap – a view echoed in America by Ross Wetzteon (*Village Voice*), who labelled the play an 'intellectual sham'. Others who faulted its central premise were Helen Dawson (*Plays and Players*, Sep 1973) and Robert Cushman (*Observer*, 29 July 1973). Certain psychological critics also became upset. Martin Gottfried (*Women's Wear Daily*, 16 Jan 1974) was disappointed with what he considered old-fashioned Freudianism in the piece, while John Simon spilled his usual vitriol, calling *Equus* hollow (*New York* magazine, 11 Nov 1974) and railing against the homosexual elements he thought he perceived (*Hudson Review*, Spring 1975). Meanwhile, psychiatrists were uniformly critical, seeing in *Equus* an

attack on their profession (Sanford Gifford in the *New York Times*, 15 Dec 1974, and in the *International Journal of Psychological Psychotherapy*, 5, 1976).

3. Psychiatrists have repeatedly attacked Shaffer for his unflattering portrait of their profession. He insists that he was even-handed: 'I think I played absolutely fair with both the doctor and his patient in *Equus*. Alan was not shown as happy, ecstatic, safe in his self-created Heaven whilst more responsible figures dwelt in a Hell of routine and prosaicism. On the contrary, he was shown as enduring dreadful nightmares every night. The penalty he paid for his excessively Dionysiac behaviour was all too clearly demonstrated. But Dysart's weary distaste for his own over-safe (over-sane, if you like), undaring life was also a legitimate emotion to display' – interview with Michael Riedel, 'The Royal Hunt of the Playwright', *Theater Week*, 2 Apr 1990, p. 31.

4. All quotations from *Equus* are taken from *The Collected Plays*, as are excerpts from Shaffer's Preface. Page references are given in parentheses following quotations.

5. Shaffer adamantly denies ever downplaying the part Dexter played in the drama's success, declaring recently again, 'I thought John's production of *Equus* was superb' (Riedel interview, p. 31).

6. 'There is in me a continuous tension between what I suppose I could call the Apollonian and the Dionysiac sides of interpreting life, between, say, Dysart and Alan Strang' – Peter Shaffer, as quoted in Brian Connell's interview 'The Two Sides of Theatre's Agonized Perfectionist', *The Times*, 28 Apr 1980, p. 7.

7. For commentary on the set see C. J. Gianakaris, 'Theatre of the Mind in Miller, Osborne, and Shaffer', *Renascence*, xxx (1977) 33–42.

8. 'The Struggle: John Dexter in an interview with Gordon Gow', *Plays and Players*, Nov 1979, p. 15.

6. 'Amadeus': Shaffer's Supreme Achievement

1. Alexander Pushkin's *Mozart and Salieri* (1830), a two-scene play, served as the basis of Nikolai Rimsky-Korsakov's one-act opera of the same title (1898). Talk of Salieri's confessions was rampant during the early 1820s, and is mentioned even in Beethoven's notebooks.

2. Publicly, Shaffer finds positive things to say concerning his key part in the making of Forman's enormously successful movie *Amadeus* (New York: Harper and Row, 1984). Privately, however, the playwright confesses himself still sceptical about translating stage plays into films. See C. J. Gianakaris, 'Drama into Film: The Shaffer Situation', *Modern Drama*, XXVIII (Mar 1985) 83–98.

3. *Amadeus*, the original soundtrack recording, performed by the Academy of St Martin-in-the-Fields, directed by Neville Marriner (two-record set, US catalogue No. WAM-1791, Fantasy, Inc., Berkeley, Calif., 1984).

4. C. J. Gianakaris, 'Fair Play? Peter Shaffer's Treatment of Mozart in *Amadeus*', *Opera News*, 46 (27 Feb 1982) 18, 36. See also Peter Shaffer, 'Playing Homage to Mozart', *New York Times Magazine*, 2 Sep 1984, p. 22.

5. Most outraged by the portrayal of Mozart was James Fenton of the *Sunday Times* (18 Nov 1979), who thought it 'appalling' and filled 'with a dreadful and offensive banality'. Michael Billington (*The Guardian*, 5 Nov 1979) also took Shaffer to task for distorting Mozart's unhappy life. A few other critics (B.A. Young, *Financial Times*, 5 Nov 1979; John Barber, *Daily Telegraph*, 5 Nov 1979; and

John Simon, *New York*, 29 Dec 1980) had other grounds for complaint.

6. All quotations from *Amadeus* are taken from *The Collected Plays*. Page references are given in parentheses following quotations.

7. Interview with Brian Connell in *The Times*, 28 Apr 1980, p. 7.

8. Unpublished interview with C. J. Gianakaris, July 1980.

9. Peter Shaffer, 'The Set', preceding *Amadeus* in *The Collected Plays*, p. 481.

7. 'Yonadab': Variations on a Favourite Theme

1. Irving Wardle in *The Times* (6 Dec 1985) admires sections of *Yonadab* for 'spectacle of the utmost virtuosity'; he also voiced reservations: 'the real objection to the play is that it lays claim to ultimate questions of man's place in the universe and reduces them simply to a theatrical structure'. Comparable remarks were made by John Peter in the *Sunday Times* (8 Dec 1985) and by Benedict Nightingale in the *New York Times* (22 Dec 1985). Other critics expressed more enthusiasm. Jack Kroll, writing in *Newsweek* (13 Jan 1986), openly admired *Yonadab*, admitting, 'For me, this is Shaffer's most daring, most personal, most honest play.' John Barber in the *Daily Telegraph* (6 Dec 1985) singled out the wit of *Yonadab*, declaring that 'Shaffer also writes the funniest of comedies'. He added that 'The huge imagination of Peter Shaffer is one of the glories of the modern stage'.

2. Preface to *'Lettice and Lovage' and 'Yonadab'* (Harmondsworth Penguin, 1989) pp. vii–viii. Shaffer states

here that at least 80 per cent of the dialogue was rewritten for the revised script. All quotations from the revised version of *Yonadab* are taken from this edition; page references, prefixed *Y*, are given in parentheses following quotations.

3. In the National Theatre programme book for *Yonadab* Shaffer acknowledges a large debt to Dan Jacobson's *The Rape of Tamar*. My quotations from the novel are taken from the original American edition (New York: Macmillan, 1970). Page references, prefixed *RT*, are given in parentheses following quotations.

4. During the week of previews in London (1985) Shaffer had to ask Wendy Morgan, the actress portraying Tamar, to keep the character from becoming a simplistic Electra figure.

5. Act II, fls 48–9, typescript, which he kindly allowed me to consult. Subsequent quotations from the original version are from the same souce.

6. See 2 Samuel 13:30–6.

8. 'Lettice & Lovage': New Comedy for a New Age

1. *Lettice & Lovage* is another of Shaffer's playful titles. In act II, Lettice Douffet explains the derivation of her name: 'It comes from Laetitia – the Latin word for gladness. As a vegetable it is obviously one of God's mistakes – but as a name it passes, I think' – *Lettice & Lovage* (New York: Harper and Row, 1990) p. 45. The term 'lovage' is defined later in the play (p. 57) as an herb of the parsley sort. All quotations from the play are taken from the Harper and Row edition, in which the author slightly altered the title by changing the 'and' to an

ampersand. Page references are given in parentheses following quotations.

2. For a closer look at the play see C. J. Gianakaris, 'Placing Shaffer's *Lettice and Lovage* in Perspective', *Comparative Drama*, 22, 2 (Summer 1988) 145–61.

3. Shaffer originally had a different setting in mind for the accidental wounding of a character who is acting out historical charades. In my discussions with the author during the play's opening week (Oct 1987) he stated that *Lettice & Lovage* derived from two initial ideas for a play and an unperformed (and unpublished) one-acter. The two ideas evolved into the first two acts of *Lettice & Lovage*, while the one-acter became the third act. The one-act play centred on a young married couple, and, though the circumstances of the accident were similar in *Lettice & Lovage*, the context was entirely different. The one-acter opened with a young man, his head heavily bandaged, sitting in a courtroom at the Old Bailey. He fumed while his wife testified about the unfortunate injury he had received during one of their private enactments of historical incidents. Just as in *Lettice & Lovage*, the couple were forced to reveal embarrassing details about the event, since a serious injury had turned their innocent pastime into a legal matter.

4. Shaffer's strong views on post-war architecture reflect majority public opinion in Britain. The leading critic has been Prince Charles, who in speeches to architects and civic planning groups late in 1987 described the situation in London in blistering terms: 'You have to give this much to the Luftwaffe. When it knocked down our buildings, it didn't replace them with anything more offensive than rubble. We did that.' And he added, 'In the space of a mere 15 years, in the 60's and 70's, your

predecessors as planners, architects and developers wrecked the London skyline and desecrated the dome of St. Paul's' – cited in Paul Goldberger, 'Should the Prince Send Modernism to the Tower?', *New York Times*, sec. 2, 13 Mar 1988, p. 33. Interviewed for the 'Talk of the Town' column in *New Yorker* (2 May 1988, p. 28), the Duke of Gloucester offered much the same appraisal: 'Strictly from an architectural point of view, it is true to say that the Luftwaffe did less damage than did the real-estate developers of the nineteen-thirties and fifties'. The crusade continues; see for example 'Whose Britain is It?' *Newsweek*, 13 Nov 1989, pp. 84–6.

5. See for instance Jack Richardson, 'The English Invasion', *Commentary*, Feb, 1975, pp. 76–8; Joan F. Dean, 'Peter Shaffer's Recurrent Character Type', *Modern Drama*, XXI, no. 3 (Sep 1978) 297–305; and Michael Billington, 'Divining for a Theme', *Guardian*, 5 Nov 1979, p. 11.

9. Speculations – Present and Future

1. These two plays suffer from other weaknesses, at least in the versions originally staged. Given that the revised *Shrivings* is verbose, we can reasonably assume that the original *Battle of Shrivings* was even more bombastic. It was also muddy thematically, and so, to a lesser extent, was the version of *Yonadab* performed at the National Theatre, London. Another weakness of the original *Yonadab* was its exaggerated spectacle, which seemed to press beyond the theme's allowable limits. Regrettably, the revised *Yonadab* has not yet (1990) been staged, though the script is excitingly theatrical. The 'Helpers' introduced in the revised version are generic,

archetypal figures comparable to the horse figures used so effectively in *Equus*.

2.   Unpublished taped interview with C. J. Gianakaris, New York, 23 Mar 1990.

3.   Quoted from Shaffer's unpublished typescript, which he graciously allowed me to consult.

4.   Interview, 23 Mar 1990.

5.   Sheridan Morley, 'Cheers for Maggie Smith', *Playbill: The National Theatre Magazine*, 30 June 1990, p. 12.

6.   I was with Shaffer when he received news of Dexter's death on 23 March 1990.

Chronology of Premieres

The Salt Land (television play)
8 November 1955 – ITV, London

The Prodigal Father (radio play)
14 September 1957 – BBC Radio, London

Balance of Terror (television play)
21 November 1957 – BBC Television, London
27 January 1958 – CBS Television, New York

Five Finger Exercise (stage play)
16 July 1958 – Comedy Theatre, London
2 December 1959 – Music Box Theater, New York

The Private Ear (stage play, presented with *The Public Eye*)
10 May 1962 – Globe Theatre, London
9 October 1963 – Morosco Theater, New York

The Public Eye (stage play, presented with *The Private Ear*)
10 May 1962 – Globe Theatre, London
9 October 1963 – Morosco Theatre, New York

The Merry Roosters Panto (holiday mime entertainment)
17 December 1963 – Wyndham's Theatre, London

The Royal Hunt of the Sun (stage play)
7 July 1964 – National Theatre at the Chichester Festival Theatre (production transferred to the Old Vic Theatre, London)
26 October 1965 – ANTA Theatre, New York

Black Comedy (stage play)
27 July 1965 – National Theatre at the Chichester Festival Theatre (production transferred to the Old Vic Theatre, London)
12 February 1967 – Ethel Barrymore Theatre, New York (with *White Lies*)

White Lies (stage play, presented with *Black Comedy*)
12 February 1967 – Ethel Barrymore Theatre, New York
21 February 1968 – Lyric Theatre, London (revised version entitled *The White Liars*)

The Battle of Shrivings (stage play revised as *Shrivings* in 1974)
5 February 1970 – Lyric Theatre, London

Equus (stage play)
26 July 1973 – National Theatre, at the Old Vic Theatre, London
24 October 1974 – Plymouth Theatre, New York

191

Peter Shaffer

Amadeus (stage play)
2 November 1979 – National Theatre, London
17 December 1980 – Broadhurst Theatre, New York

Yonadab (stage play)
4 December 1985 – National Theatre, London

Lettice and Lovage (stage play)
27 October 1987 – Globe Theatre, London
25 March 1990 – Ethel Barrymore Theatre, New York
  (revised version entitled *Lettice & Lovage*)

Whom Do I Have the Honour of Addressing? (radio play)
May 1989 – BBC Radio, London

Select Bibliography

All sections except those listing full-length studies and critical articles (which are in alphabetical order by author or title) are ordered chronologically.

Published Playtexts

Five Finger Exercise
London: Hamish Hamilton, 1958
New York: Harcourt Brace, 1959
Harmondsworth: Penguin, 1962 (revised version, in *New English Dramatists, 4*)
Harmondsworth: Penguin, 1968 (in *Three Plays: Shaffer, Wesker, Kops*)
Harmondsworth: Penguin, 1976 (in *Peter Shaffer: Three Plays*)
New York: Harmony Books, 1982 (in *The Collected Plays of Peter Shaffer*)

Peter Shaffer

The Private Ear
London: Hamish Hamilton, 1962 (with *The Public Eye*)
New York: Stein and Day, 1964
London and New York: Samuel French, 1964
Harmondsworth: Penguin, 1981 (in *Peter Shaffer: Four Plays*)
New York: Harmony Books, 1982 (in *The Collected Plays of Peter Shaffer*)

The Public Eye
London: Hamish Hamilton, 1962 (with *The Private Ear*)
London and New York: Samuel French, 1962
New York: Stein and Day, 1964
Harmondsworth: Penguin, 1981 (in *Peter Shaffer: Four Plays*)
New York: Harmony Books, 1982 (in *The Collected Plays of Peter Shaffer*)

The Royal Hunt of the Sun
London: Hamish Hamilton, 1964
New York: Stein and Day, 1965
New York: Ballantine, 1966
London: Samuel French, 1968
London: Longman, 1968 (Study Text)
London: Pan, 1969
New York: Harmony Books, 1982 (in *The Collected Plays of Peter Shaffer*)
London: Longman, 1983
(Opera libretto by Iain Hamilton) Bryn Mawr, Pa.: Theodore Presser, 1982

Black Comedy
New York: Stein and Day, 1967 (as '*Black Comedy, including 'White Lies'*)

194

London: Samuel French, 1967 (with *White Liars*)
London: Hamish Hamilton, 1968 (with *White Liars*)
New York: Samuel French, 1968 (revised and rewritten)
Harmondsworth: Penguin, 1981 (in *Peter Shaffer: Four Plays*)
New York: Harmony Books, 1982 (in *The Collected Plays of Peter Shaffer*)

White Lies / The White Liars / White Liars
New York: Stein and Day, 1967 (as *Black Comedy, including 'White Lies'*)
London Samuel French, 1967 (*White Liars*, with *Black Comedy*)
London: Hamish Hamilton, 1968 (*White Liars*, with *Black Comedy*)
London and New York: Samuel French, 1976 (revised, as presented in 1976)
Harmondsworth: Penguin, 1981 (in *Peter Shaffer: Four Plays*)
New York: Harmony Books, 1982 (in *The Collected Plays of Peter Shaffer*)

Shrivings (the original *The Battle of Shrivings* was never published)
London: André Deutsch, 1974
New York: Atheneum, 1974 (in *'Equus' and 'Shrivings'*)
Harmondsworth: Penguin, 1976 (in *Peter Shaffer: Three Plays*)
New York: Harmony Books, 1982 (in *The Collected Plays of Peter Shaffer*)

Equus
London: André Deutsch, 1973
New York: Atheneum, 1974 (in *'Equus' and 'Shrivings'*)

Peter Shaffer

London: Samuel French, 1974
New York: Avon, 1975
Harmondsworth: Penguin, 1976 (in *Peter Shaffer: Three Plays*)
New York: Harmony Books, 1982 (in *The Collected Plays of Peter Shaffer*)
London: Longman, 1983

Amadeus
London: André Deutsch, 1980 (first version, premiered in London)
New York: Harper and Row, 1981 (revised text)
Harmondsworth: Penguin, 1981
New York: Harmony Books, 1982 (in *The Collected Plays of Peter Shaffer*)
London: Longman, 1984 (Study Text)
London: Methuen, 1985 (in *Landmarks of Modern British Theatre II: The Seventies*)

Yonadab (original version never published)
Harmondsworth: Penguin, 1989
Harmondsworth: Penguin, 1989 (in *'Lettice and Lovage' and 'Yonadab'*)

Lettice & Lovage (ampersand replaces 'and' in title in 1990 edition)
London: André Deutsch, 1988 (original version)
London: André Deutsch, 1988 (revised edition)
London: Penguin, 1989 (in *'Lettice and Lovage' and 'Yonadab'*)
New York: Harper and Row, 1990 (as *Lettice & Lovage*)

The Collected Plays of Peter Shaffer
New York: Harmony Books, 1982 (the only collected-works volume available at present)

Select Bibliography

Novels and Other Prose Works

The Woman in the Wardrobe (London: Evans, 1951). Published under the pseudonym 'Peter Antony'.

How Doth the Little Crocodile? (London: Evans, 1952; New York: Macmillan, 1957). Co-authored with Anthony Shaffer; English edition published under the pseudonym 'Peter Antony'.

Withered Murder (London: Gollancz, 1955; New York: Macmillan, 1956). Co-authored with Anthony Shaffer.

'But my Dear' and 'The President of France', in *That Was the Week That Was*, ed. David Frost and Ned Sherrin (London: W. H. Allen, 1963).

Film Scripts

Lord of the Flies (1963). Script (based on the novel by William Golding and co-authored with Peter Brook; not filmed).

The Public Eye (1972). Script based on Shaffer's one-acter; film sometimes distributed under the title *Follow Me!*

Equus (1977). Script based on Shaffer's play; nominated for an Academy Award.

Amadeus (1984). Script based on Shaffer's play; winner of an Academy Award.

Unpublished Writings

The Salt Land (1955). Television play.

The Prodigal Father (1957). Radio play.

Balance of Terror (1957). Television play.

The Merry Roosters Panto (1963). Christmas entertainment.

Whom Do I Have the Honour of Addressing? (1989). Radio play, to be published by André Deutsch, London.

Full-length Studies of Shaffer's Work

File on Shaffer, compiled by Virginia Cooke and Malcolm Page (London: Methuen, 1987).

C.J. Gianakaris (ed.), *Peter Shaffer: A Casebook* (New York and London: Garland Publishing, 1991).

Dennis A. Klein, *Peter Shaffer*, Twayne English Authors (Boston, Mass.: G. K. Hall, 1979).

Gene A. Plunka, *Peter Shaffer: Roles, Rites, and Rituals in the Theatre* (Rutherford, NJ: Fairleigh Dickinson University Press, 1988).

John Russell Taylor, *Peter Shaffer*, Writers and their Work (London: Longman, 1974).

Shaffer's Own Commentaries

'Labels Aren't for Playwrights', *Theatre Arts*, XLIV (Feb 1960) 20–1.

'The Cannibal Theatre', *Atlantic Monthly*, CCVI (Oct 1960) 48–50.

'In Search of a God', *Plays and Players*, Oct 1964, p. 22.

'To See the Soul of a Man', *New York Times*, sec. 2, 24 Oct 1965 p. 3.

'*Equus*: Playwright Peter Shaffer Interprets its Ritual', *Vogue*, CLXV (Feb 1975) 136, 192.

'Scripts in Trans-Atlantic Crossings May Suffer Two Kinds of Changes', *Dramatists Guild Quarterly*, Spring 1980, pp. 29–33.

'Salieri Was Really the Only Choice', *New York Times*, sec. 2, 14 Oct 1984, p. 8 (letter).

Published Interviews with Shaffer

Joseph A. Loftus, 'Playwright's Moral Exercise', *New York Times*, sec. 2, 29 Nov 1959, pp 1, 3.

Mel Gussow, 'Shaffer Details a Mind's Journey in *Equus*', *New York Times*, sec. 2, 24 Oct 1974, p. 50.

Tom Buckley, 'Why Are There Two U's in "Equus"?', *New York Times Magazine*, 13 Apr 1975, p. 20 ff.

Brian Connell, 'The Two Sides of Theatre's Agonized Perfectionist', *The Times*, 28 Apr 1980, p. 7.

Roland Gelatt, 'Mostly *Amadeus*', *Horizon*, Sep 1984, pp. 49–52.

Michael Reidell, 'The Royal Hunt of the Playwright', *Theater Week*, 2 Apr 1990, pp. 30–4.

Critical Articles

Tom Buckley, '"Write Me", Said the Play to Peter Shaffer', *New York Times Magazine*, 13 Apr 1975, p. 20ff.

Joan F. Dean, 'Peter Shaffer's Recurrent Character Type', *Modern Drama*, XXI (Sep 1978) 297–306.

Dean Ebner, 'The Double Crisis of Sexuality and Worship in Shaffer's *Equus*', *Christianity and Literature*, XXXI (1982) 29–47.

Roland Gelatt, 'Peter Shaffer's *Amadeus*: A Controversial Hit', *Saturday Review*, Nov 1980, pp. 11–14.

C.J. Gianakaris, 'A Playwright Looks at Mozart: Peter Shaffer's *Amadeus*', *Comparative Drama,* XV (Spring 1981) 37–53.

——, 'Drama into Film: The Shaffer Situation', *Modern Drama*, XXVIII (Mar 1985) 83–98.

——, '*Lettice & Lovage*: Fountainhead of Delight', *Theater Week*, 2 Apr 1990, pp. 22–5.

——, 'Shaffer's Revisions in *Amadeus*', *Theatre Journal*, XXV (1983) 88–101.

Brendan Gill, 'Bargaining with God', *New Yorker*, 29 Dec 1980, p. 54.

Jules Glenn, 'Alan Strang as an Adolescent: A Discussion of Peter Shaffer's *Equus*', *International Journal of Psychoanalytic Psychotherapy*, (1976) 473–87.

——, 'Twins in Disguise: A Psychoanalytic Essay on *Sleuth* and *The Royal Hunt of the Sun*', *Psychoanalytic Quarterly*, XLIII (1974) 288–302.

Michael Hinden, 'Trying to Like Shaffer', *Comparative Drama*, XIX (Spring 1985) 14–29.

Werner Huber and Hubert Zapf, 'On the Structure of Peter Shaffer's *Amadeus*', *Modern Drama*, XXVII, 299–313.

Dennis A. Klein, '*Amadeus*: The Third Part of Peter Shaffer's Dramatic Trilogy', *Modern Language Studies*, XIII (1983) 31–8.

Barbara Lounsberry, 'God-Hunting: The Chaos of Worship in Peter Shaffer's *Equus* and *The Royal Hunt of the Sun*', *Modern Drama*, XXI (1978) 13–28

Gene A. Plunka, 'The Existential Ritual: Peter Shaffer's *Equus*', *Kansas Quarterly*, XII (Fall 1980) 87–97.

James R. Stacy, 'The Sun and the Horse: Peter Shaffer's Search for Worship', *Educational Theatre Journal*, XXVIII (1976) 325–37.

Russell Vandenbroucke, '*Equus*: Modern Myth in the Making', *Drama and Theatre*, XII (Spring 1975) 129–33.

Doyle W. Walls, '*Equus*: Shaffer, Nietzsche, and the Neuroses of Health', *Modern Drama*, XXVII (1984) 314–23.

Index

Index